Essays on the Poetry of Stephen Gill
Anthology of Critical Papers and Articles

Essays on the Poetry of Stephen Gill

Anthology of Critical Papers and Articles

Edited by

Shaleen Kumar Singh

ADHYAYAN

ADHYAYAN PUBLISHERS & DISTRIBUTORS

New Delhi-110002

Published by
ADHYAYAN PUBLISHERS & DISTRIBUTORS
4378/4B, 105, J.M.D. House, Murari Lal Street
Ansari Road, Darya Ganj, New Delhi - 110002
Ph.: 011-23263018, 011-23277156, Fax: 23280028
Email: adhyayanpublishers@yahoo.com

Essays on The Poetry of Stephen Gill
Anthology of Critical Papers and Articles

Edition 2010
ISBN 978-81-8435-119-4

Printed in India

Published by Harish Chandra Yadav for Adhyayan Publishers & Distributors, Delhi. Laser Typesetting at V. M. Graphics and Printed at Tarun Offset Printers, Delhi

Acknowledgement

The editor is deeply thankful to the following publication in which a few chapters of the book have appeared previously:

The Stephen Gill Gazette online

The editor pays his heartfelt thanks to Stephen Gill for his constant motivation, all round support and skilled guidance in the completion of the work.

RAVANAS OF TODAY

When I read
children disappearing inside the blackness
limbs scattered
and mothers crying
every speck of me
falls apart.

Maniac messiahs
play diatribe songs
on an impaired piano
of their design.
The abrupt harshness
of their discordant sounds
come from the notes of treasons.
These Ravanas and Kamsas
pollute the air of serenity
in the Flame
with arrows of their insanity
that end in the emptiness
of the nadir frustration.

Where is the daybreak
of the source
that ends the melodrama
of the dark force
I simply ask.

– *Anuradha Sharma*

Foreword

Dr. Gill is a prolific writer whose work in prose and poetry enjoys considerable renown. He is talented and wide-range in his literary span. His works have earned recognition in the field of literature both at home in Canada and internationally. I wish him well in his efforts to utilize poetry as a conduit to peace for humankind. I am glad to recommend him to the reading public, particularly to those who have a love for poetic writing and universal peace.

Dr. Hirsch L. Silverman
West Orange, NJ
USA

Preface

The poetry of Stephen Gill deserves serious attention by critics, primarily because it is about *satya* (Truth), *dharma* (righteousness), *shanti* (peace), *prema* (love) and *ahimsa* (non-violence). These five watchwords of the Upanishads are the foundation stone of the most ancient document of Indian philosophical wisdom. In *satya* or *truth,* one can seek the fulfillment of the quest of intellect. In *dharma* or *righteousness,* one can confirm the will and get the inspiration to the right conduct. In the basic attitude of *shanti* or *peace,* one can find the resolution of the welter and conflict of human emotions. *Prema* or *love* is nothing but the awakening of the soul and the steady flow of intuition and *ahimsa* or non-violence is refreshing from causing harm through one's vision, hearing, talking or action. These five pillars of Upnishadic philosophy yield the five great ideals – knowledge, skill,balance, insight, vision and spirituality.

Gill's poetry also aims at the installation of these ideals in man's thought and action. As an exemplary idealist poet, he has composed a good number of long and short poems to relay his message of unity among the citizen of the world. He excels other poets due to his unflinching faith in goodness, simplicity, relevance and communication. His canvass is wide and his conception is deep.

His poetry has reached not only the foremost nook of the earth but also to the innermost recesses of his reader. In his comprehensive interview to Nilanshu Kumar Agarwal,

Dr. Stephen Gill comments, "Poetry is experience that can happen anytime with or without reason." In the light of above statement it can be said that the poetry of Stephen Gill is the fresh rosary of varied beads of experiences woven with the reason of peace and without the reason of 'self-enhancement' or 'self propagation'.

Dr. Stephen Gill has always believed in the tradition of Sufism. Sufism is an ancient school of wisdom which puts emphasis on basic unity of the underlying ideals in all religions and mystic schools considering love as the first and foremost principle. According to Hazrat Inayat Khan, a great Sufi master of India, "Sufism is not a new religion or community; ... it is an attitude of life." He adds, "It is like viewing from airplane a town, the streets of which one has known and walked through and yet one has seen the whole town at glance." Similarly the poetry of Gill provides a graphic glance of the present-day world and suggests 'love' as the first religion of man to be followed by uprooting the weeds of hate and terrorism from the hearts and sowing the seeds of hopes and aspirations.

My short but intimate relation with the poet has made me realize that he is both a man of letters and a man of parts coupled with higher human values in his life.

He and his poetry are drenched in the mystical waters of Sufism. I remember Sudhir K. Arora who has compared his poetry to the poetry of Khalil Gibran and has written:

> If Khalil Gibran had been alive today he would have certainly written on terrorism. If Gill had not experienced the pain and misery of destructive forces, he would have certainly written on the secrets that might open the key to a successful life that ultimately makes man spiritual.

Like Gibran, Gill has successfully exposed the horrors of violence, shaping a key to open the doors for a life of peace. Just for this, Stephen Gill deserves the ultimate accolade. The message of Gill is love and its propagation among his fellow beings. With his selfless motive, Gill has served the Muse, propagated love and peace that has excelled him among the poets of the world.

Essays on the Poetry of Stephen Gill is a collection of exhaustive articles by different scholars of the world. I have attempted to cover all major themes of Gill's poetry by collecting critical leanings of serious scholars. I am grateful to each for his/her insightful ruminations and judicious judgement. Above all, I think of Stephen Gill with great reverence for his blessings and invaluable succor that I have received frequently from him. His meaningful cooperation and skillful guidance in the completion of the book is beyond my expression. Meeting with Daisy Verma, the Associate Professor in the Dept. of English, H.P. University Regional Campus, Dharamshala, was a turning point for me as she introduced me to Dr. Virender Parmar, another practicing poet and critic of repute. She prayed Dr. Parmar on my behalf to write the foreword of the book. I am failing in words to pay my heartfelt thanks to both of them. I must pay deep thanks to Dr. Kalpna (my wife) for her all round support and also to Ruchi and Aakansha for lending me a helping hand. I am also grateful to Harish Yadav of Adhyayan Publishers for moulding these critical papers in the shape of a lively book.

Last but not the least, I am thankful to Lalita Singh, my mother, for her ever-flowing love, Saurabh Singh, my elder brother and his wife Madhu Singh for providing me an amiable atmosphere to learn and study.

Shaleen Kumar Singh

Introduction

On being questioned in an interview as to why he writes, Stephen Gill answers: "I use to reincarnate myself to live peacefully in my home that is poetry". Living in his peaceful abode of poetry, the poet emphatically voices his concern for global peace, social security and universal brotherhood. He preaches the gospels of love, knowledge, and compassion. Such an attitude is a pure and complete participation mystique when one comes to accept the 'itness of things'. It is the cultivation of a higher and finer stage of consciousness when the narrow, confined self awakes to experience the vast comic self. This is an emergence of the human ego from its limited enclosed sphere of a pond to an open, free expanse of a river which flows towards a union with the sea. But at the same time, his vision of such a world may sound idealistic and platonic and utopian. Like every great author, he has certain dreams and he is as he himself says in the same interview set on a "never ending journey for a horizon that is non-achievable". He struggles through words to accomplish and to fulfil what he sincerely aspires for. The origin of his dreams can be traced in his childhood when deprived and denied of stability and security, he had to move from one place to another and ultimately land in Canada. Any other person with such young age turbulence would have turned biased and prejudiced against the world or even life itself but Gill maintains a harmonious ego self-axis and never lets disintegration or disorientation take precedence. Rather he transcends the narrow shell of individuality and ontologically traverses the 'I-Thou' matrix of relationship and thus reaches the state which Karl Jasper describes as 'being-in-itself'. Despite the flux of time and vicissitudes, he is firm and resolute in his convictions. He nurtures, cherishes, and nourishes certain hopes, desires and dreams, yet he is never oblivious of the contemporary reality.

The poem 'The Flame' bears a testimony to the fact of his creative responsiveness to the present world scenario. However, he never opts to talk of his subjective and unpalatable and unsavoury early life experiences, yet many a time they crawl unconsciously and inadvertently in his works. Like a remarkable quester, Gill is a traveller of a destination where not the fool but the rigours and hazards of the road matter. No doubt many have travelled but only a few have reached, yet the achievement of those who couldn't reach cannot be undermined because of perseverance and relentlessness. Hemingway said, "A man may be destroyed but not defeated." And Gill is not the one to accept defeat. He has become a name and a voice, distinct and unambiguous. A look at the awards and recognitions he had achieved is like an iceberg whose major dimensions and magnitude is invisible. Apart from four honorary doctorates and Laureate Man of letters, he got Sahu award of honour plaque from the world council of African churches, Pegasus international poetry for peace award, the Best poet of peace award for the year 1993 and the Queens' Golden Jubilee medal. In order to appreciate his real worth and genius as a poet one has to go to his works which include the following volumes of poems titled *Shrine* and *Songs before Shrine* which include *Reflections and Wounds, The Dove of Peace, Song for Harmony, Divergent Shades, Flashes* (trilliums in Haiku Spirit) and The *Flame.* He has also authored three and a few short story books apart from critical studies on H.G. Wells, W.B. Yeats and G.B. Shaw. He has written books in Urdu, Punjabi and Hindi, also edited few books and taken up works in translations. Prominent singers have put his poems to music and scholars have tried to discover him as a man and as a author in the critical studies namely *Glimpses, Stephen Gill and His Works* and *Discovering Stephen Gill*. The above resume, howsoever brief presents the potentials of an author who with his work in English, Panjabi and Hindi has fascinated the imagination of the readers in its own way. With amazing insights and creative energy which spring from within, he reveals his poetic prowess to acquaint us with his depth, variety, magic and prolificity.

An international man of letters, Gill has a wide range of interest in mythology, philosophy, spirituality, history, politics, and above all man and the world he lives in. The numbness, pain and anguish of the human mind and soul and the inscrutable human world portrayed in his poems tempts mysteriously the reader to plung deeper. His poetry opens the infinite world of beatitude along with damp dungeons of suppression, violence and contempt. Imbibing creative and artistic flavour, the emotions present themselves symbolically and via irony and sympathy land at a realistic plane. His poetry that churns and sieves intricate human issues some time would tickle us to smile at others which makes our eyes wet but certainly it compels us to ponder and to contemplate. With its uninhibited unrehearsed and exhilarating spontaneity of expression, he chalks out the myriad vistas of human life to present a collage of variegated sense and sensibilities that animate our daily existence. He has already made a mark to find favour with both the Indian and overseas reading public. His perambulation both in the familiar and unfamiliar zones and the conscious and the unconscious chambers of human psyche touch the chords of emotions with the penetrative power of reaching out to the core of others being. 'The Flame' the longest poem ever written in English on the theme of terrorism reveals the poet's 'aliveness' to the world around him. The title of the poem is symbolic with layers and layers of meanings. It stands for the evil that surface in a man with its diabolic powers to destroy all that is good, noble and worth living. It may mean a creative bonding energy man and man, man and God. It may also be purgatory fire that consume passion and sensuality opening vistas of spiritual realms "to weed out the spite/ the dark/the frowning evil/ the war/ the misery/ the hard days/ and for dialogue to guide/the good to lead". Similarly his other poems present subtleties to decipher new meanings, interpretations and thus escape final analysis. The pervading violence, bloodshed and gloom which come with terrorism and do not shake the poet's faith in the inherent goodness of man. Like Yeats he expects a revelation a Second Coming to restore the disturbed order. He employs a simple diction but it is pregnant with certain nuances of creative and positive suggestiveness. His imagery is a beautiful painting of words. It is illustrative and communicative in nature. It makes us to pause, to ponder and to contemplate.

Thy feet rest in the waters
But the mouth is parched
Near ripples I lie
Both solitary sides
Stare at the bank tearfully
To kiss each others' dry lips
While the waters flow by.

Gill's poems come across as fresh breeze of morning a range of emotions and thought qualifying him for the status of a post- modern poet. His apprehension and acute awareness of the contemporary world and its problems is remarkable. He seeks harmony and coherence amid all that is irksome, chaotic or tumultuous and spreads the message of love, the gospel of integration, altruism and agape. As a poet he shows maturity and purposiveness—one who is fully conscious of the physical world and at the same time having a perception of the larger dimension of issues found in the metaphysics. Many a time the issues under poetic surveillance are left inconclusive and unresolved; it is precisely this which gives thrust, impetus and strength to Gill's poetry. What is commendable throughout his works is the clarity of thought, command over diction, colloquial simplicity and above all his conviction in what he writes and the courage to uphold it.

Dr. Virender Parmar
Department of English
Himachal Pradesh University
Regional Centre, D'sala

List of Contributors

Anandam, K., a Lecturer in English, VHNSN College is specialized in Indian writing in English and ELT. He has undertaken a study on "Teaching English for Technical and Non-Technical students" for his Ph.D. research. He has published articles on ELT and Diasporic poets.

Arora, Sudhir, a poet and critic, teaches English at Maharaja Harishchandra Post-Graduate College, Moradabad. He has co-edited a book on Girish Karnad. His publications include, *A Study of Kamala Markandeya's Women, A Thirsty Cloud Cries* and *A Key to Literary Terms and Forms.* He has recently written a book and also edited a collection of critical essays on Stephen Gill.

Baskaran, C., is Reader in English, VHNSN College, an affiliated institution of Madurai Kamaraj University, Madurai. He has put up 21 years of teaching and research experience which helps him to guide 10 scholars to get their Ph.D. and some 12 are working in Indian Writing in English and Commonwealth Literature Studies. He has published a book titled *Narrative Desires: Colonial and Postcolonial Novels on India,* and he has submitted two books for print. He has also published articles and essays in referred journals and books. At present he is working on a UGC sponsored project on "Gender Relations in Mahesh Dattani's Plays".

Choudhary, Arbind Kumar edits *Kohinoor,* an international journal of creative and critical writings. He is the head of the department of English at R.C. College in Bihar, India. He has authored collections of poems including *Eternal Voices, Universal Love* and *My Songs.*

Gill, Stephen is Poet Laureate of Ansted University and an Adjunct Professor of EAU. He is an expressive voice of Canada, India and Pakistan. He believes strongly in a democratically elected world government and peace through peaceful means. Gill has authored more than twenty books, including novels, literary criticism, and collections of poems. His poetry and prose have appeared in more than five hundred publications, mostly in Canada, the United States of America and India. Stephen Gill has received awards and recognitions, including four honorary doctorates. At present, he is an honorary member of the Ansted University Board of Advisory Council, a director of the Children's Aid Society of the United Counties of Stormont, Dundas & Glengarry (Canada), and advisor to several publications. He has appeared in prestigious national and international reference books. Stephen Gill was born in Sialkot, Pakistan, where he passed his early childhood and grew in India. After teaching in Ethiopia for three years, he migrated to England before settling in Canada.

Hussain, Shujaat is a prolific and celebrated book reviewer, eminent literary critic, sensitive poet and creative author of eminence. He is widely anthologized and honoured with several national and international accolades. More than 45 literary journals have carried his write ups, available on many web pages and his works have been translated into several foreign languages and regional languages.

Kala, S.J. is Senior Lecturer in English at Fatima College, Madurai (India). She is doing her Ph.D. on Stephen Gill. Her areas of interest include Canadian Studies, English Language Studies, Mass Communication and Journalism.

Kumar, Ashok is Reader and Head, Department of English, Feroz Gandhi College, Rae Bareli. He is a genuine scholar and critic of repute. He got his D. Phil. from University of Allahabad in 1993. He has to his credit the book *The Novels of Manohar Malgaonkar*. The book shows his sharp critical insight in literature. Presently he edits *Impressions,* a journal of contemporary literature.

Prime, Patricia is a poet, critic and reviewer from New Zealand. She is the co-editor of New Zealand haiku journal *Kokako* and review-editor of the ezine *Stylus*. She is honoured with Poet of the Millennium award by the international Poets Academy in 2001. She has collaborated with fellow New Zealand Haijin, Cathirine Mair, on the two books of loiked verse, *Sweet Penguin* and *First Ray of the Sun*. She has written essays on the Contemporary Indian English Poetry and on Australian poetry.

Rajput, Kalpna is the poet, translator, reviewer and the co-editor of *Creativesaplings*. She has been widely published in India and abroad. Her Poems articles and papers have appeared in different journals of India and abroad. Her publications include *Pearls of Wisdom (Vol. One), Pearls of Wisdom (Vol. Two) and Pearls of Wisdom (Vol. Three).* Her research areas include Women Studies and Indian Literature.

Savio, G. Dominic is Reader in English at The American College, Madurai. He is a renowned author and scholar with three books and countless articles to his credit. Besides, he has travelled abroad on various fellowship programmes. His research interests are Comparative literature, Indian literature, Canadian literature, Translation Studies and Woman's studies.

Sharma, Anuradha is a Lecturer in English at Navjivan Arts and Commerce College in the state of Gujarat. She is a creative writer and critic. Her poems and articles have appeared in many reputed magazines and books.

Shama, Brhama Dutta (b.1942) retired as Professor and Head, Department of English, Kumaun University, Nainital. He was also the Director of the DSB Campus at Nainital for about nine years. Prof. Sharma was awarded Ph.D. and D.Litt. degrees on his work on John Updike and the Beats respectively. He has authored numerous articles on various global poets of the east and the west. He is the author of *Essays on English Literature, Essays on American Literature, A Spiritual Vision in John Updike's Early Fiction, Ecology* and *Oriental Philosophies in Beats, Contemporary Indian English Novel* (co-author), *The Dancing Straws* (a collection of his poems in English), *Neerav Kone Se* (a collection of his poems in Hindi). Currently he is Professor of English, Taiz University, Yemen.

Sharma, Nar Deo is a distinguished poet and stylistician who outshines the new generation of Indian English poets and critics. He is an eminent linguist, critic, translator, and teacher. His masterpiece monograph *Style in the Manneristic Poetry – Flickers* written in scholarly, inimitable style has established him in the literary world and his poetry collection *Melody of Wounds* was highly discussed among critics.

Singh, K. P. is presently working as Lecturer in English (Selection-Grade) in Professional Communication at the Department of Applied Sciences & Humanities in Kanpur Institute of Technology, Kanpur. His Research and teaching experience exceeds the span of more than five years during which he has taught courses related to communication, literature, language and human values at both graduate and postgraduate level. His areas of interests are Indian Writing in English, Indian Aesthetics and Literary Theory and Criticism.

Singh, Shaleen Kumar is the Chief Editor of *Creativesaplings,* an online Journal. He has to his credit a number of critical papers on Indian English poets and novelists. He has edited a number of books of Poetry and Criticism. Recently his maiden collection of poetry *Proprietary Pains* has been published from Poets Printery, South Africa.

Contents

1

Significance of Foregrounding in Stephen Gill's Poetry

Nar Deo Sharma

Stephen Gill is a renowned, qualitative poet and his English poems stand out from that of other modern poets on account of foregrounding of intense sensibilities, precision of expression, creative imagination, symbolic use of language and liltingly vivid imagery. I have attempted to make an essay of various linguistic deviations that have enhanced the quality of poems compiled in his two poetry books: *Songs Before Shrine* (2007) and *The Flame* (2008).

Known as the pioneer of New Criticism, John Crowe Ransom has rightly stated: "Honest criticism and sensitive appreciation is directed not upon the poet but upon the poetry". To concur with Ransom's sweeping statement, Stephen Gill's deviant style in poetry is interpreted in this critique. Poet's remarkable linguistic inventiveness 'involves both extra freedom (including freedom to depart from the rules of grammar) and extra discipline (the discipline which comes with the superimposition of special structure on language)' - G.N. Leech et al., *English Grammar for Today.*

It is the specific style that cultivates emotive spell in poetry. Style is the totality of exclusive linguistic choices systematized effectively in poetry. The systematization of linguistic choices comprises of sentences, clauses, neologism, word music, creative imagery, and symbolic import. Stylistic analysis is description, explication and evaluation of literary style.

By way of stylistic analysis, the significance of foregrounding or linguistic deviations is justified which largely contributes to figurative and symbolic use of language and adds to the novelty of expression in poetry. In the 'Preface' of the poetry book *Songs Before Shrine*, the poet has not only deliberated upon his painful, bitter experiences but also the vitals of texture in poetry. The poet maintains that "the language of poetry is more compact, energetic, of greater intensity and emotional depth than the language of prose is .... poetry needs revisions for perfection". Gill's poetry mirrors his poetic precepts. Peace, fraternity and love are the thematic sinews of Gill's poetry.

The starting poem "To Mother" carries the foregrounding of affectionate pathos apparent in these lines, "I see your tearful eyes/and catch the chocking moans/coming from the crumbling pyramid of pains/ shroud is spread/on my despair". In these lines, alliterative metaphorical phrases—"crumbling pyramids of pains...... shroud spread on despair" carry lexical or semantic deviation inasmuch as words of incompatible features have been collocated against the selectional restrictions rules of semantics. Every word testifies distinctive linguistic features as contrasted and analysed as under:

Pyramid		**Pain**
+	concrete	+ abstract, - concrete
+	countable	- countable (suffering of mind or body)
-	human	+ human
-	animate	+ animate
-	emotive	+ emotive

	Shroud		*Despair*
+	concrete	-	concrete, + abstract
+	countable	-	countable
-	human	+	human
-	animate	+	animate
-	emotive	+	emotive

It is obvious that intangible feelings are concretized by collocating the words of clashing features sorted out above which accounts for semantic foregrounding but it clarifies the intensity of meaning.

Thus linguistic deviations amounting to symbolic use of language cause brevity and novelty of expression. The semantic deviation caused by the association of words having opposite features suggests that as the vast structure of pyramids is razed with harsh, grating noise, so death wrings the soul out of body with ineffable pain. Shroud typifies the pall of death over despair and it connotes that bereft of mother's affectionate prop the poet presumes himself to be a breathing corpse.

There are 81 poems in *Songs Before Shrine* and every poem is worthy of reading. Here only those important poems are interpreted which outshine others in connection with lexical deviations or foregrounding, intensity of feelings, beautiful picturesque imagery and symbolic richness. Peace is the recurrent theme of poems. In the beautiful poem "The Dove of Peace", the poet has systematized subtle lexical resources of refrain, contrast, internal rhyme, irony of situation, sarcasm and symbolic imagery. These lines recur three times in the poem.

For a long time
I have been hearing
the dove of peace will be freed
shortly·

The recurrent refrain reminds how the politicians dangle

the cherished prospects of maintaining permanent peace, but the monsters of sham politics dally with the sincere feelings of the public and replace the inevitable peace by the frenzied dance of mass killings of innocent people. The macabre spectacle of political terrorism is juxtaposed in these lines to show how the motif of peace is shrugged off:

Cannons have been installed
over dead bodies
flesh famished weapons have flown
dirge-chanting vultures set free
robots thirsty now for more blood
and the Animal of Hostilities
is preparing the last dance
many more maimed
lofty dreams crushed.

Judicious animal imagery is exercised to expose the brutal behaviour of the terrorists. The alliterative metaphoric phrase "flesh-famished weapons" connotes the disgusting vacuum of humane attributes and vampire thirst in terrorists. The term 'robots' tagged to terrorists implies their role as machines meant for the destruction of humanity.

Our homes now better adorned with thorns of hatred.

The above two lines carry symbolic import, grammatical and semantic foregrounding and lexical polysemy or multiple meaning that are analysed under:

homes *(noun)*	(i) + concrete, - human, + countable
	(ii) Dwelling places, nations
	(iii) Reservoirs of humane feelings; (symbolic, thematic meaning)
adorn *(verb)*	(i) + concrete, - human, + countable
	(ii) cultivate (thematic meaning)

thorns *(noun)* (i) + concrete, - human, + countable
(ii) annoying attitude
(symbolic, thematic meaning)

hatred *(noun)* (i) - concrete, - countable, + human,
(ii) violent dislike

According to semantic rules, the verb "adorn" requires a noun having + concrete, + count, - human features like medals, pictures, flowers, statues but not *hatred*. These lines attract syntactic deviation and connote that some nations propagate violence and abhorrence in people instead of peace and love. Linguistic deviations or foregrounding at various levels come to question when lexical items are placed in abnormal combinations in violation of the conventions of language. Poet's objective of introducing linguistic deviations in his poetry is to foreground his unique experience which cannot be described in ordinary language. The following exemplary lines occurring in the poem "Harmony" speak volumes for the effectiveness of linguistic deviations, figurative use of language and foregrounding of felicitous phrases:

For the culture of dialogue
harmony weaves fabrics
to womb the fetus of wisdom.
Harmony
the author of prosperities
compose a sonata
for the piano of delight.

As a commendable potpourri of the varieties of linguistic deviations, the poem "The Meechlake Fish" shines with wonderful foregrounding of disgusting violence. Foregrounding lies in the deliberate deviation from the established conventions of language usage. Foregrounding means the use of any device of language in such a way that its deviant use itself attracts attention and is perceived as uncommon. Pore over the following lines to examine and enjoy the marvels of foregrounding.

With a tail for deliberate ruin
a crocodile of racial disharmony
enters the waters of my land

It plays with the waves of life
muddying the crystal flow of love

Fear and ignorance carry how
explosives of confused hatred

One can see red drops
sailing with morning bubbles
shaped like graves.

Here the gleanings of vivid foregrounding are elaborated. The abstract adjectival phrase *racial disharmony* pre-modified by the concrete noun "crocodile" brings about semantic deviation, but such deviant collocation of lexical items has foregrounded the ugliness and fierceness of racial disharmony causing a heavy toll of innocent lives.

The peculiar grammatical device "enallage" is apparent in the redesigned word *muddying* in that the root form of adjective 'muddy', which denotes stagnant dirtiness, is restructured into present participle by affixing inflectional suffix-ing to adjective *muddy*, and the deviant form of present participle 'muddying' implies the terrible situation which reflects unremitting defilement of love by hate. Metonymy exercised in the coordinated phrase *fear and ignorance* suggests that timid and illiterate persons were forced to truckle to the detonation of strong hate against mankind in the fiendish role of terrorists.

Another metonymic phrase *red drops* postmodified by the simile phrase *shaped like graves* demonstrates the traces of the trail of massive massacre that can be observed in the horrible scene of blood-smeared dead bodies floating in the river. The significance of foregrounding originating from various linguistic deviations is transparent in above lines which contribute to economy of expression with remarkable novelty.

In the poem "Man of Today", a rhetorical question is framed and placed at the end of poem as a nuance to identify the mercurial nature of modern man.

Subtle stylistic devices, such as, parallelism, foregrounding of hypocrisy, syntactic coherence and judicious contrast of clashing situations have been exercised by the poet to judge the unpredictable, volatile character of modern man. An inventory of controversial and deceitful practices of modern man is presented in series of equivalent contrasts of agonizing outcome.

Syntactic Foregrounding

Contrastive equivalence of prepositional phrases

Constructive prospects		*Destructive deeds*
On the one hand		*On the other*
songs for peace	↔	distribution of weapons
On the one side		*On the other*
refuge for sufferers	↔	death from starvation
On the one hand		*On the other*
slogans for freedom	↔	the nights of cruelty
appeals for love	↔	the fire of hatred
crises for unity	↔	thirst for blood.

It is noteworthy that the convergence of prepositional phrases at equivalent positions as pre-modifiers and post-modifiers in addition to the ellipsis of subject and verb-phrases highlights effectively the contemptible breach of promises by treating the extremities of double dealings by modern man. Stephen Gill deserves hearty praise since he has not given room to diction dirt like slang, jargon, archaism, cliches, vulgarism, but he has threaded his poems with fresh, decent, emotive and symbolic imagery.

In his other commendable poetry book *The Flame*, Stephen Gill has garnered the rich harvest of the odyssey of his woes. *The Flame* is an excessively long poem painting the massive human destruction wrought by terrorists— the maniac messiahs. It contains eight parts branched out into 62 cantos. Peace, the keynote of the poem, is disrupted by the mercenary demons of death. Flame flashes multiple shades of meanings. Flame typifies the surge of exuberant energy of life. Flame connotes the warmth of affections, patriotism, fraternity, knowledge, divine faith. On the contrary, flame reflects murderous perversity in context of terrorists. With vile metaphors, the poet has slashed terrorists. Review the array of derogatory metaphors capping their barbarity : "monster of perversities", "avatars of savagery", "locusts of threats", "fanatic howls", "vultures of blood-shed", "snakes of personal migraines", "sullen zealots", "artisans of insidious shocks", "trotting arm savages", "inglorious advocates of wicked designs", and "poisonous belligerents".

The Flame is a mosaic of simile, metaphor, metonymy, personification, antithesis, oxymoron, hyperbole, allusions, symbols, sarcasm, picturesque imagery, linguistic deviations and foregrounding. In the first part, the poet has eulogized the graces of God that have animated every element of nature. Figurative diction, word music and picturesque imagery and personified nature add beauty to these lines:

You flower a fragrant feast
caress
the flushed cheeks of the horizon
the keenness of insight
beats within the hyacinths
of your smile.

A few lines clustered with linguistic deviations effectively reveal how the beauty of nature and innocent people are destroyed by the brutal terrorists:

the avatars of savagery

mow down defenceless innocents
spiders of sinister news
crawl in and out of the cracks
of the tranquil trust.
From the bushes of disharmony
leaves fly around
and fall in the pond of mistrust.
Wounded kids were crying on the grass
and broken bodies
discarded like hot dog wrappers.

Symbols are employed in great abundance. A symbol is defined in the *Princeton Encyclopedia of Poetry and Poetics*, 1986 in these words: "A literary symbol unites an image (the analogy) and an idea or conception (the subject) which that image suggests or evokes".

Most important significance of symbols is interpreted in these words: "An idea which would be difficult, flat, lengthy, or unmoving when expressed prosaically and big itself, may be made intelligible, vivid, economical and emotionally effective by the use of symbols." A symbol is a "pseudo-subject". Metonymy plays very significant and pronounced role in the figurative and symbolic use of language in poetry. According to G.N. Leech, "Metonymy, on the semantic level, is transference of meaning". Metonymic word is an abstract noun but it is made tangible by associating it with a concrete noun clause.

According to Kenneth Burke, abstract and spiritual words are metonymic in origin. Mostly metonymic phrases or words are skipped from interpretation because of their covert meanings. Metonymic phrase "the cracks" signifies the persons who fall away from loyalty, and "leaves" also typifies traitors. Figurative uses of language contribute to various linguistic deviations. According to Leech, "Linguistic deviation is the waiving of rules or conventions of language". In fact, a poet perceives certain similarity in dissimilarity and he combines words of dissimilar features.

In metaphoric phrases, "sinister news", "tranquil trust"

"bushes of disharmony", and "pond of mistrust", words of concrete and abstract features, are combined in order to create novelty of thought, economy of expression and emotive punch.

Other remarkable feature of Gill's deviant style lies in the use of grammatical innovation "enallage" (Scott, 1971) that is, the interchange of one part of speech for another, as noun for verb, verb for noun, etc., and functional conversion. Leech maintains that functional conversion consists in adapting an item to a new grammatical function without changing its form. Alliterative remarkable sentence *You flower a fragrant feast* carries functional conversion or enallage. Basically the grammatical category of the word *flower* is noun, but its syntatic function is of a verb in this sentence.

It can be discerned that functional conversion causes economy of expression inasmuch as verbal function is implied also in a noun. The word *flower* effecting two-fold functions of a subject and a predicate interprets the message of object as follows:

You flower a fragrant feast (enallage)

subject	*verb*	*object*
Flowers subject	flower verb	a fragrant feast object

It is suggested through *enallage* or *functional conversion* that God serves a feast of fragrance culled from fine flowers. Symbolic language knits fresh and novel imagery and Gill is pastmaster in dressing his intense feelings with symbolic imagery which underscores these lines:

The smooth surroundings
of the temple of my flame
have grown treacherous
in a thickening fog

These lines comprise of the convergence of metonymy

and metaphor. The metonymic phrase *the temple* symbolizes piety or devotion to God and good works. Metaphoric phrase "a thickening fog" connotes the overwhelming milieu of fanatic storm that precipitates a person to revel in an absolute frenzy of human destruction.

Poems contained in part six-- cantos 26-31—have outweighed others on account of intensity of foregrounded sensibilities, symbolic language, sensuous imagery, felicity of inventive phrases. With novelty of symbolic diction, the poet has juxtaposed the heavenly atmosphere in canto 28 where innocent people dwell silently and peacefully, and the satanic attributes of terrorists indulged in massive massacre.

Here stood
the sanctuary of the lofty art
of tender awareness
where life veiled in the ineffable sanctity
flourished.

The adherents of a wicked belief
left a dent with the claws
textured in the laboratory of their conceit.

The ashes ask
why the blind brutes
draw no boundary for their hailstorms.
The streets wandered forlorn for days.

On account of semantic deviation, the poet has foregrounded the vile role of terrorists in these sentences and phrases: "Wicked belief" connotes frenzied fanaticism. Scientific metaphor *laboratory* with - human, -animate, +concrete features is collocated with + human, + animate, -concrete featured word 'conceit'.

Semantically deviant sentence suggests that obsessed with the extremity of vain pride of fanaticism, the terrorists have ruined the peaceful, loving life of common people by means of their blasting rage. Metonymic phrase "the ashes" associated with human, animate feature verb *ask* suggests the petrified conscience of the terrorists who do not hesitate in dibbling their bayonets in the delicate bodies of innocent children. Again the metonymic phrase as subject – "the streets" presupposes the horrible situation that people did not walk in streets for many days as curfew confined them in their houses to adhere to precautionary safety measures against bomb blast carnage by terrorists.

In canto 43, the poet details the allegory of the birth of a terrorist. Innocent, poor youths are terrorised first then traded into the crime of human destruction as these symbolic lines reflect the reality:

I see a deer chased
by a tiger who is fed
on the flaunting fruits of terror
in the bushes of unparalleled ignorance
where he cannot hear
the birds of freedom.

Animal and botanical images are exercised to define the shameful breeding of terrorism. Deer typifies an innocent, simple youth, while tiger signifies a savage supreme leader of terrorism. The metonymic phrases *the bushes of unparalleled ignorance* suggests that the illiteracy, poverty, shocking miseries of a great number of youths are merchandized and channellized into terrorism.

Cantos 10 to 31 display catalogue poems that lay bare exhaustive inventories of the massive destruction of human beings and invaluable properties:

Many lost their eyes
ears and fingers
bones broken and twisted
rambled in shock
among the debris and dead bodies
broken bodies
discarded like hot dog wrappers

to set up
a makeshift morgue
where a truck
refrigerated the slaughtered.

They removed the nursery
buried under a pile of rubble
a pyramid of ashes
over the cradles
days were filled with funerals...

Rhetorical question as a refrain "Who can tell" is repeated thirteen times in order to pry into the terribly offensive attitude of fanatic desperadoes and a few lines are very conspicuous because of symbolic import and innovative imagery:

Who can tell
how they felt
tormenting the bird of peace
with the cigarette lighter of their lust
or the butt of the rifle of their bigotry.

Metaphoric innovative phrases, *Cigarette lighter of their lust* defines terrorists as cruel and depraved rape-addicts. The last stanza of canto 34 bespeaks the poignant wailing for the bereaved kith and kin:

Who shall water
the dreary fields of freedoms
turn pages of hope
for battered handicaps
and prepare something daily
for them
on the fire glowing in the hearths
of emptiness.

Last four lines recall the most memorable lines of Gray's ever fresh poem *Elegy Written in a Country Churchyard.*

For them no more the blazing hearth shall burn.
Or busy house wife ply her evening care.

Apart from describing the loathsome panorama of massive destruction wrought by insane terrorists, Stephen Gill paints the exquisite beauty of his beloved (probably) with picturesque imagery in canto 42.

I feel the feathers of a rose
your presence I find inside
softly wrapped.

On the whole, the long beautiful poem serves the harmonious blend of realism, idealism and humanism in innovatively inimitable style.

It was 2008 when the poetry of Stephen Gill came to my full notice. I bought a copy of *Songs Before Shrine* from the World Book Fair held in February. The book of 81 poems are praiseworthy because they highlight the author's deep and strong sociopolitical and peace concerns. I found the preface was pithy, informative and fetching. As a poet myself and also a linguist and critic, I discerned in the poems precision and clarity of expression, picturesque description of God's serene beauty manifested in Nature which stands out in strong relief against the shoddy, chaotic human nature. I found in the collection of Stephen Gill's poems a harmonious blend of concrete and abstract imagery, in addition to compression of thoughts. Linguistic deviations and emotive foregrounding have contributed to brevity of the poet's varied experiences and also appealing figurative use of language. There was no smack of jejune prose in his long poems cast in free verse.

I agree with Dr. Ravi Nandan Sinha that

> *Stephen Gill's poetry is a pleasure to read. In his work imagery arises with inevitable naturalness leading to magnificence that is typically his own. The heterocosm created by Gill is wide and rich, full of sun and shade.*

> *It is like a lush valley of flowers gazing up at a multicoloured sky. (Divergent Shades,* 8)

Even his long poems — 28 of pages and 2 of three pages do not seek squeamish relish of sentimental sniveling and tedious, erratic dilation of poetic vision which often happens to modern poetasters who fail to differentiate emotive spell of poetry from dull prose. Good poetry caters a variety of feel-feast-meal to sensitive readers. The poems compiled in *Songs Before Shrine* buttress up Stephen Gill's preface perceptions that "poetry needs revisions for perfection... poets are professional workers who keep polishing the tools (phrases, sentences, symbols—my own interpretation) of their trade."

Stephen Gill repeats the same conviction in *The Flame,* the longest poem on modern terrorism:

> *A poet should never be tired of revisions. A time comes when a poem would tell when to stop. Sometimes poets have to stop revisions, because they get tired of what leads them nowhere, even knowing that the poem needs extra work. In such situations, I put my poem aside to take it up some other day unexpectedly. This procedure works in most cases with most poets. Often poets will know themselves if a poem needs further work. It is like knowing when the stomach is full.* (17)

Stephen Gill does not belong to any school of poets. He confesses his awareness when he says:

> *I do not belong to any school or era of poetry. My poetry is the psalm of my soul. To me, a poet is a discoverer of unknown continents through the voyage of the self. A poet is also a priest who through the mantra of poetry reaches the god within.* (17)

From his poetic concept expatiated in the prefaces and encapsulated in his poems, it can be deduced that social concerns and the cause of true peace are the strong and sterling objective correlatives in his poetry.

References

Burke, Kenneth. *A Grammar of Motives:* quoted in *Princeton Encyclopedia* of *Poetry and Poetics.*

Chomsky, Noam, *Aspects of the Theory of Syntax*, Cambridge, Mass: MIT Press, 1965.

Gill, Stephen, *Songs Before Shrine*. Delhi : Authorspress, 2007.

Gill, Stephen, *The Flame.* Montreal: Vesta Publications, 2008.

Gill, Stephen. *Divergent Shades,* India: Writers Forum, 1995.

Guerin, Wilfred et al. *A Handbook of Critical Approaches to Literature.* 5th Ed. Oxford: OUP 2005.

Leech, Geoffrey N. *Semantics.* rpt. Harmondsworth: Penguin, 1978.

Leech, Geoffrey N. *A Linguistic Guide to English Poetry*. Twelfth. imp. New York: Longman, 1987.

Leech, Geoffrey et.al. *English Grammar for Today*. rpt. London: Macmillan, 1990.

Preminger, Alex et. al. (Eds.), *Princeton Encyclopedia of Poetry* and *Poetics* rpt. London: Macmillan Press, 1986.

Scott, A.F., *Poetry and Appreciation,* rpt., London: Macmillan, 1971.

Sharma, Nar Deo. *Style in the Manneristic Poetry: Flickers,* (Monograph). Bangalore: Mrs. Chandrakantha D.Kabadi, 1995.

Atlantic Literary Review, The. "Interview with Stephen Gill", July-Sep. & Oct.-Dec., 2004, vol. 5, nos. 3-4, pages 164-183.

2

Pacifism in Stephen Gill's Poetry

Brahma Dutta Sharma

In his poetry Stephen Gill appears as a pacifist and a champion of peace and harmony. In a number of his poems, such as 'Talking of Peace', 'Light of Truth', 'Divided Humanity', 'About War', 'The Gulf Crisis on TV', 'A Familiar Scene', 'If There Be a Third World War', 'Prayer for the Coming Years', and 'To Be' he describes wars as occurrences causing destruction and peace and harmony as the bringers of happiness, growth and construction. He explicitly says that a war is an undesirable occurrence. For example, in his poem 'Prayer for the Coming Years' he says that he wishes to weed out war:

Strengthen me with thy Manna
to weed out
the war
the misery
and the hard days of the past
and to help
good to emerge
in the coming years (DS 9)

The poet wishes to have a future which is free from wars,

and misery. He regards warfare as an undesirable phenomenon. He associates peace with construction and wars with destruction. For instance, in his poem 'Hounds of War' he writes:

When
the hounds of war
ravage
the luxuriant pastures of prosperity
melodies of the dove slumber
under the foliage of the rainbow
of discontent. (*Shrine* 56)

He is asserting in this poem that wars bring harmony to its end, kill melodies and prevent people from realizing their dreams. When he says:

The dove pleads
that the dance of the hounds
be stopped
to let her pacifying carol
fortify human muscles
to build more Taj Mahals and pyramids
of justice (*Shrine* 56)

He suggests that human muscles can make justice have its sway only when there is peace.

In his poem 'War Fever' Gill lists some of the losses that war causes to humans and their surroundings:

War fever
poisons the air of surroundings
disturbs the calm of sea
crumbles human relations
kills the appetite of the soul
weakens the liver of love...(*Shrine* 49)

According to Stephen Gill, a war turns everything upside

down because it pollutes the air of the surroundings, disturbs the calm of seas, and weakens the feelings of love, spiritualism and friendship.

Gill repeatedly states in his poems that war causes mass killings. For instance, in his poem 'Trilliums' he defines war as an act of slaughtering:

War:
to buy blossom of a mother
for slaughtering of another. (*SH* 56)

In his poem "About War" he writes:

War creates more widows
renders infants fatherless
sets homes in darkness
and loses human affection. (*SH*- 22)

He draws his readers' attention to the other harms that wars cause. For example, in the same poem:

War pollutes the air
making life very hard
it produces untold terrors
and stocks tearing tensions. (SH 22)

If one is sensitive to human misery one must feel pity for a woman who has become a widow whether she belongs to our country or to that of our enemy. Likewise, a boy who has lost his father has been deprived of the care one gets from one's father, with the result that he has been rendered pathetic.

A human child needs care for a long time and unless proper care, including education, is made available to him, he remains deprived of an opportunity to develop his talents properly. When the poet says, *War pollutes the air* (see *supra*) he draws the readers' attention to another problem. The air we breathe in is highly polluted and it needs efforts to control the level of pollution. Since wars increase pollution, they should not be allowed to occur.

The fourth problem to which the poet draws our attention is that wars make life hard as it causes a lot of destruction and deprives people of what they have created to make life less hard. Since it is in the interest of the survival of human race, life should be made as easy as possible. What makes life hard must be looked upon with askance. When the poet says that a war *produces untold terrors* (see *supra*), he is drawing attention to the fact that during the days of war nothing is safe and any city, any man and any building may be targeted any time.

It is still fresh in the memory of mankind that during the Second World War, Hiroshima and Nagasaki had been targeted by the USA and the World Trade Centre of the USA was targeted by the terrorists of the Middle-East on the 11 September 2001. When the poet says that a war *stocks tearing tensions* (see *supra*), he is drawing attention to the fact that one can be targeted any moment, one cannot be at ease and will find oneself full of tensions most of the time. In a number of his poems Gill gives pen-pictures of the victims of fighting and brings into focus the damages which the wars cause. For example, his poem 'The Gulf Crisis on TV' is replete with such pen-pictures:

Women crying
around debris
men hurling abuses
children confused and despaired
the Patriots intercepting the Scuds
the showers of bullets
downing the planes, and
the bombs piercing through homes.(Shrine 55)

The pictures of women crying around, broken buildings, men expressing their rage against an aggression, and children not even able to understand what is happening are indications of the havoc that a war causes.

A parallel settings have been painted in 'A Familiar Scene' in which the bodies of slain soldiers and the other victims of war are lying discarded in garbage and rolling in ditches as there is none to perform their last rites:

Bodies rolling in ditches
or dumped with the garbage.
Bodies washing up
on to the beaches
like bundles of clothes
or lying discarded
in open mass graves
heaped together
in grotesque piles. (Shrine 68)

It is immensely pitiable that the bodies of the soldiers who have died for their country have been left uncared for.

Gill does not remain contended with this but goes to say that when these people were alive they had their dreams, aspirations and visions. They were not inanimate or thoughtless. Their dreams and aspirations have also died with them:

In half-shut eyes
Their dreams are now stones,
Bodies wrapped with red
Lie in the lap of dust (*Shrine* 69).

It is the dreams of people that make them work to make shining achievements in life. For example, Milton had a dream that he would leave behind him a poetical work of such merit that people "will not let it willingly die". He realized this dream when he wrote his epic *Paradise Lost.* Gill writes in the same poem 'A Familiar Scene':

Here is a mother
who moves the corpses
to find her son;
here is the cry of an old man
buried in the cries of the wounded. (*Shrine* 69)

It has been suggested that wars make the dependents of the victims helpless because they are left without a bread-earner and therefore dependents have to lead a life of deprivation. The sight of a mother trying to identify the body of her son among the corpses lying uncared for and an old man crying for his son are pathetic.

Gill does not keep himself confined to the sufferings of unidentified people only. He writes also about people who have been identified. For instance, in 'Somali Victim of 1992 Tribal Warfare' he narrates the story of a boy who is admitted to a hospital. He illustrates the condition of the boy in the following words:

> *he has not eaten for days*
> *it may be his rapacity*
> *for the food of the village*
> *or because he gave up hope.*
> *Life has not yet crept back*
> *into his sight.*
> *He may not remember*
> *his days at home*
> *because of fever*
> *and constant headaches.* (*Shrine* 73)

This boy is a victim of the tribal warfare:

> *When*
> *the tribal smoke of animosity*
> *overshadowed the smiling landscapes*
> *of Somalia*
> *his father lost everything* (*Shrine* 75).

In the following lines, there is a suggestion that the boy is not likely to survive:

> *The nurse says*
> *swollen limbs mean*
> *the case is desperate.*

A famished body
eats its own fat
and finally protein for energy.
Muscles weaken,
weakening the heart. (*Shrine* 75)

This is tantamount to saying that what happens during warfare may uproot families, may cause them financial losses, and may even wipe them out from the face of the earth. Gill adds further:

Around him lay
emaciated, rag-clothed kids.
Some have swollen bellies
and some sores on their heads,
hands or feet (*Shrine* 74).

It is obvious that this boy is not the only victim of war. There are several who share his fate. Gill shows the effects of warfare also on cities. For example in 'Bride is Watching' he illustrates how a war converts Karachi, once a bride-like city, into a slaughter-house:

Her lap has become
a slaughtering spot
with the swords
that had sheltered her home. (*DS* 43)

Stephen Gill rejects the assertions of the people who idealize war, because it gives the victor a glory, it is fought for the progress of the nation, it ends misrule, it stops corruption, or it settles disputes. In 'About War' he says:

Don't tell me
war is a winning glory
it is to defend the land
and stop regression.

Don't tell me
war is boosting pride
it is to end misrule
and to stop corruption. (SH 21)

If wars are that bad, war-mongers must be regarded as the tools of the forces of evil rather than those of the forces of light. That is the reason why Gill describes war-mongers as the persons getting sustenance from the land of darkness. He says in 'Light of Truth':

War-mongers are drinking
from the land of darkness.
The land of devils is empty
because its occupants
extend desert of savagery...(DS 47)

Akin to them are the arms traders whom Gill regards as insane when he says:

Sleeping in the web of greed
arms traders forget the dove
hidden in the caves of blood.
Appearing in the stage of the future
the coming generations will go insane
thinking of their insanity. (Shrine 50)

In his poem 'Reptiles', Gill tries to identify the feelings which are inimical to peace and harmony. He asserts that they are fanaticism and racism:

...a fanatic reptile
...hides among the shrubs
where the flowers of peace
cannot bloom" (SH 47).

He calls the dungeons of racism cold and loveless when he says:

In those sunless lands –
Cold dungeons of racism –
birds cannot fly" (SH 47).

Even in his poem 'Evening of Harmony', he regards racial prejudices as the enemies of peace. He says:

... the night of racial prejudice
chews peace
in the jaws of endless depth (SH 48).

Gill wants pacifism to be accepted as a principle when he draws his readers' attention to the fact that if there is one more World War, it may cause the annihilation of the whole mankind. He describes it in his poem 'If There Be a Third World War' in which he writes:

If another war breaks out
no one may survive
to watch white front of the moon
that is often so fascinating
and to sit in pleasant warmth
of the sunshine...
seasons may come and go
but no singer to glorify them. (SH 23)

The onus of establishing peace in the world, according to Gill, is not only on rulers but also on leaders, statesmen and even on ordinary citizens. He expresses this opinion in his poem 'Talking of Peace'.

Here he reminds the people of these categories of what they have been doing to damage the cause of peace. He finds it hypocritical on the part of rulers to talk of peace when they have armed their countries with nuclear weapons to the teeth.

He laments:

Our rulers talk of peace

but it is futile
when nuclear-powered marines
sail over breasts of the oceans;
missiles look down
and neutrons
make fun of every life. (Shrine 46)

The implication is that rulers can be sincere in their efforts for peace only when they adopt disarmament as a matter of policy. Gill expects politicians, in case they are sincere in their efforts for peace, to enable citizens not to be intimidated by murderers as he says in this poem 'Talking of Peace':

Our politicians want peace
but it cannot be achieved
as long as citizens are locked
in the prison of their fears;
their daily bread,
doled out by murderers,
and love worshipped
with bullets. (Shrine 46)

Gill wants leaders to free people from tensions of human relations, to remove their ignorance, and to see that their basic needs are gratified as he writes:

Our leaders
envision peace
but it can never be real
if homes are destroyed
by tensions of human relations;
the arteries of ignorance
continue hardening
and the merciless locusts
of the basic needs
keep buzzing
over individuals and lands. (Shrine 47)

The implication of the statement is that real peace can be attained only when family life is free from tensions, people are no more ignorant and their basic needs are gratified. He may be saying so in view of the fact that if the inhabitants of a country find it difficult to gratify their needs, they tend to attack other countries. Gill expects also common citizens to work for peace. He expects them to shorten the arms of darkness to reduce the heaps of arsenal and to get rid of pollution. This is what he means in this poem:

Our citizens
crave peace
but it shall remain a dream
because
the arms of darkness grown longer;
the crop of the arsenal is raised
and the demons of pollution
stand tormenting us. (Shrine 47)

Gill also wants criminals to be punished and autocrats be stopped from dominating citizens:

Everyone
discusses peace
but it leads nowhere
when there is no accounting
of criminals;
and the subjects are dominated
by the cruelty of the autocrats. (Shrine 48)

No doubt, disarmament can free the world from the fear of an armed war, but no single country can be expected to disarm itself as nobody can assure it that it shall never be attacked.

Poet is right when he shows how wars cause deaths and destruction but there remains the question as to what a victim of wrongs should do in order to stop the hand of the wrong-doer, in case he resolves not to fight. Gill should have made a distinction between a war to rob and a war to escape from being robbed. The second kind of war cannot be regarded as unjustifiable. There have been thinkers who have rejected the use of weapons to achieve one's end, but they have offered alternatives. For example, Thoreau offered the path of passive resistance as an alternative to an armed resistance. Mahatma Gandhi resorted to the use of non-cooperation in his fight against the British rulers of India in the pre-Independence days. But Stephen Gill does not suggest any alternative to an armed struggle against injustice and tyranny. Nor does Gill takes up the question as to what victims of racism and fanaticism should do to stop racists from oppressing them.

References

A. Primary Sources

Gill, Stephen. *Divergent Shades*. Ranchi: Writers' Workshop, n.d. (abbreviated as *DS* in the text).

—— *Shrine: Poems of Social Concern*, Benson: World University Press, 1999.

—— *Songs for Harmony*. Cornwall: Vesta Publications, 1992 (abbreviated as *SH* in the text).

B. Secondary Source

Glimpses: A Selection of Published Articles about Stephen Gill and His Books, Cornwall: Vesta (Canada), 1999.

3

Disjunctive Social Processes in Stephen Gill's *The Flame*

G. Dominic Savio and S.J. Kala

> *If a man does not make new acquaintances as he advances through life, he will soon find himself alone...."*
>
> *(Samuel Johnson)*

An individual abhors the state of isolation. He is not born into this world to live a life of segregation. From womb to tomb he/she continually interacts with other members of the society to fulfil his/her needs. This spurs an individual to come in contact with other members of the society. Society comprises of norms and statuses—the static element and it includes social interaction, the dynamic element too. No individual is spared of social relationships, the functional aspects of society. They are engaged in different kinds of interaction called social processes. The term "Social Process" encompasses human interaction and patterns of behaviour. According to Green, social interaction is

> *"...the mutual influences that individuals and groups have upon one another in their attempts to solve problems and in their striving toward goals. Social interaction discloses the*

concrete results of striving behavior upon roles, statuses, and moral norms" (Green 57).

He also elaborates that "social processes are merely the characteristic ways in which interaction occur" (Green 57). Social interaction that takes on a specific direction evolves into a social process. Social processes are found in all societies. The processes of interaction have been classified by sociologists based on the relationships that exist between two interacting individuals and groups. "So classified the forms of interaction are called the social processes" (Biesanz 113).

Integrative or Associative or Conjunctive social processes and Disintegrative or Dissociative or Disjunctive social processes are the two kinds of social processes. "Those processes which tend to create harmony or unity in society" are called Integrative or Associative or Conjunctive social processes (Ruhela 133). Accommodation, adjustment, assimilation, cooperation and integration fall under this category. Those processes "which tend to create disharmony or disunity in society" (Ruhela 134) are Disintegrative or Dissociative or Disjunctive social processes. They are competition, conflict, contravention and dissension. Literature also mirrors these Conjunctive and Disjunctive processes. Like many literary works Gill's works too talk of these social processes.

Stephen Gill, a Sialkot born, Indian-bred, multiple-award winning writer in Canada has authored many collections of poems, fiction, literary criticism, and the books of historical nature. His writings throw light on his deep passion for Global peace and social concerns. His undying thirst for peace seeps through one of his recent publications, *The Flame* (2008), a long poem about the destruction caused by maniac messiahs.

The Flame is about peace and peace is the main area of my exploration" (*The Flame* 19). This long poem which is an outcome of Gill's eight years of work is divided into eight parts that are further divided into sixty two cantos. In Gill's own deliberation on the poem, the first part of *The Flame* is devotional. The second, third, fourth, fifth are about the destruction caused by maniac messiahs. The sixth part deals with those responsible for destruction. The yearning for the loss surfaces out of the seventh and eighth part of the poem. Hope reigns in the last part of the poem.

A close study of the poem, *The Flame*, exposes the fact that a major portion of the poem deals with the causes and consequences of disjunctive social processes. Hence, the paper aims at identifying the type of disjunctive process, studying their specific characteristics and analysing their positive and negative effects on the society.

Gill's *The Flame* mentions many socially defined relationships and specifies certain social processes. Though social processes involve both conjunctive and disjunctive processes yet, the poem brings into focus only the disjunctive processes. With social contact and communication being the essential conditions of social processes, it is scrutinized that negative social contact that paves the way for unhelpful social processes are predominant in the poem. "The adherents of a wicked belief" (95) communicate only "wanton violence" (100) in the poem.

Before delving deeper into the social processes, a study of the two essential conditions - social contact and communication - of social processes becomes obligatory. What sort of social contacts are underscored in the poem? Before that what is a social contact? It is a pair of *social actions* that have no further consequence. Social contacts can otherwise be called an accidental *social interaction*. "social actions refer to any *action* that takes into account the actions and reactions of other *individuals* and is modified based on those events" (Social Action, Wikipedia).

As social contact can be called an accidental social interaction, in Gill's *The Flame* the social contact that takes place is due to the explosion of the Day Care Centre. The social interaction among the victims' parents, the volunteers, the fire fighters, other rescue operators, doctors, nurses and counsellors is a social contact of a kind.

There is a social contact of a different kind. The plan chalked out by the terrorists with the mastermind of the blast preceding it, is certainly a type of social interaction. The scheming is also an interaction between human beings as Max Weber has pointed it out. It takes place in windowless cells.

> *... in the windowless cells*
> *of anarchistic gospel*
> *they prepare terror (The Flame* 104)

The terrorists are trained to carry out the project and they are sufficiently brain washed to execute the task. It vouches for the social contact among them. The social contact leads to a social action, the blast that in turn leads to actions and reactions of other individuals in the society. Their alleged actions and reactions are modified based on those events.

> *A camp was extemporized*
> *in a parking lot....*
> *The area was cordoned off*
> *most exit ramps were closed....*
> *Investigators and relatives*
> *filled the hotels.*
> *Hospital postponed planned surgeries*
> *and nonessential radiological*
> *procedures. (The Flame* 81)

The alleged reactions that are modified because of the social action are manifested in the above lines. With the study of the first condition of social process, social contact, an investigation of its next condition - communication — is indispensable. The learned skill, communication, is acquired by different people in varied ways for innumerable purposes. In Gill's *The Flame* the people that we come across can be broadly classified into two types. Firstly, the afflicted, their friends, relatives and rescue operators in general can be grouped together. Secondly, they are the maniac messiahs, the source of all affliction. Both groups of people use only oral communication in the poem.

A look at the first group of people, tells that they orally communicate with one another only in their anxiety to trace someone alive or dead or to help one another in some way or the other.

A woman
showed a picture of her two sons
to everyone to know
if they had seen them....
Another,
requested all
if they had spotted her daughter. (*The Flame* 77)

The maniac messiahs' terrific act, though unsaid, certainly involves communication. They in their secret hideouts would undoubtedly have drawn out specific details about the safe implementation of the devilish deed, debated again and again about its feasibility. Who knows it might have involved even some written communication? Whatsoever it may be they have openly communicated hatred for humanity through a violent act. These conditions pave a way for social processes. Of the four social processes – competition, conflict, contravention and dissension that create disharmony or disunity in the societies– conflict abounds in *The Flame.*

"Conflict is deliberate attempt to oppose, resist or coerce the will of another or others" (Green 58). In *The Flame,* there is no situation of cold war, that is conflict in the form of threat but there is a detailed description of violence and its repercussions. If it is so, what type of a conflict is it?

Simmel has spelt out four types of conflict. They are war, feud, litigation and conflict of impersonal ideas. The violence in *The Flame* is not clearly the implication of a war, a feud or litigation. Nor is it an eruption of conflict of impersonal ideas that is carried on by the individuals not for themselves but for an ideal. No one in the poem seems to be fighting for an ideal.

...the social lepers wander
among the denominations of malice

brazen about their endless idols
to worship the bubbles
of the self. (The Flame 99)

There is yet another typology of conflict that can be classified into corporate and personal conflict; latent and overt conflict; class conflict; racial conflict; caste conflict; group conflict; and international conflict. The verbal pictures of violence and its aftermath featuring in *The Flame* can be identified as a corporate conflict or a group conflict. The violence described does not talk about just an individual or a group being a victimized, but it talks of the killing of a great number of people:

When
the avatars of savagery
mow down defenceless innocence. (The Flame 48)

The line "mow down defenseless innocence" brings out the image of a lawn being mowed by a mower in an attempt to maintain it. Gill with his apt choice of words brings out the appalling predicaments of the innocent victims of the disaster wrought by the maniac messiahs.

The crumble of steel doors
besmear with red drops.
Pressed into a shaky layer
of a massive cake
stuffed with metal, broken furniture, ... (The Flame 49)

Such devastation is surely the outcome of a corporate conflict or a group conflict. "Corporate conflict occurs among the groups within a society or between two societies. Groups often attempt to impose their will upon other groups...." (Green 59). Race riots, communal upheavals, religious persecutions, labour-management, conflict and war between nations are examples of a corporate or a group conflict.

Though Gill does not talk conspicuously about the cause

of the horrifying violence, yet it is clear that it is an upshot of terrorism, a topical issue bothering everyone in the globe.

I cannot see
the burning bush of your beauty
because terrorists have loosened
suffocating gases...(The Flame 106)

The terrorists and their insane behaviours modify the behaviours of others. The terrorists act that takes place in the poem robs each individual of their peace. They are no more "citizens of peace" (*The Flame* 104)

Thick black smoke
that arises from cannons
hovered above the choicest gem
leaving the smell of the gun powder
to poison the palate of peace. (The Flame 51)

The scenes of "deafening disorder", "the waves of supreme disaster" (52) and "wanton violence" (100) in *The Flame* can also be evidences of group conflict. It is a conflict "found between two more groups of any kind ...." (Rao 320). The "avatars of savagery" (48), the "blood spillers" (89), the heartless humans who "deal with the devil", "the sightless assassins of the innocence" (90), and the "social lepers" (99), are the individuals who are in conflict with other groups of the society.

Even though the destructive act has been identified as the result of the corporate or group conflict yet the features of conflict in general can be attributed to it. In keeping with such a notion, let conflict, a disjunctive social process that has certain specific characters be analysed.

Firstly, conflict is universal. It is nothing new and unique to a society. No specific reference to a geographical location of the Day Care Centre in the poem allows Gill to assure for the universal nature of conflict. The Day Care Centre that is shattered to pieces in the poem is not of any particular city, nation, or a continent.

Children either breakfasted
or played
and the cribs overlooked the street. (The Flame 70)

Had the poet named the Day Care Centre or the street that it overlooks, the readers would have certainly distanced themselves from it and the disaster that have struck it. They might have felt just the way they would have after reading of such an incident from a newspaper. They may even breathe a sigh of relief and feel undisturbed that it has happened in some corner of the globe. But, the situation of the poem makes any reader from any part of the globe to empathize with the victims and feel for them as he would when his own friends or relatives are confronted with it.

Secondly, conflict is a conscious process. Members of a group harm the members of the other group consciously and knowingly. Gill, too is quite sure that it is a conscious process. In Part Six of *The Flame* he shoots forth a volley of questions at the assassins revealing the alertness of their consciousness before the act.

Who can tell
if they wiped sweat
before unchaining the bulldozers
of their delusional disorder ...
Who can tell
if the night before
they tied and untied the knots of reason...
(The Flame 90-91)

What more can keep one's consciousness alert other than reason? Still, they do not pay heed to it. Thirdly, sociologists are of the opinion that it is emotional. The whole process is founded on emotions.

Sociologists say that men's actions are guided by instincts and not by logic or reasoning. Gill too upholds the same idea:

Who can tell
if the tender hands of the toddlers
tried to strangle
the throat of their conscience. (The Flame 91)

The phrases "delusional disorder", "strangle the throat of their conscience", "tied and untied the knots of reason" used by Gill in the poem are instances of conflict being emotional. The terrorists are purely driven by instincts, terms Gill. Had logical thinking and reasoning accompanied the attack it would have been avoided. But, even that seems to be lacking. In the poem Gill is not quite explicit about what they wanted to achieve as he himself is not sure of it:

Who can tell
what it was
they wanted to achieve
and the glare of which beliefs
lured them
for a tango with the agents of carnage
on the mountain of emptiness. *(The Flame* 94)

Fourthly, any conflict is a personal process. The destruction of Day Care Centre, by the terrorists does not have a valid cause but, it may have a personal motive. The coming together of the individuals as terrorists is certainly because of an individual, his personal and inner unhealed wound or his consideration of it as a pastime. Gill himself is of such a belief:

...they become maniac messiahs
to snuff out the inner blaze
breathing the stink of ferocity
as a pastime (The Flame 102)

Fifthly, conflict is intermittent. Its appearance and disappearance happens suddenly. There is no proof of it being continuous. In the poem too the attack is very sudden:

Suddenly
windows came crushing in
and the ceiling began to drop. (*The Flame* 70)

The disastrous act specified in the poem is so sudden that nobody is able to recollect how it happened and what followed it like the "grandmother" who feels that she has woken up from a bad dream.

For his grandmother
it was awakening
from a bad dream. (*The Flame* 71)

Conflict, a fundamental social trait, is an inevitable part of the society. Simmel is of the opinion that conflict- free society is impossibility. Whatever be the type of conflict, it has a specific role to play in the society. It has to be underscored that it has both positive and negative roles to perform. The positive effects of conflict in general are many. But, only one of its effects that can be associated with corporate or group conflict is taken for study. "The group in conflict with another group is strengthened in its 'we' feeling" (Biesanz 116).

The rescue operations that follow the devastation bear witness to the strengthening of the bond among the victimized and the empathisers. Such a situation also paves ways for the emergence of a leader.

The leader often shouted
as loud as he could:
"We are here to help.
call out."
All would wait, praying
to hear a whisper or sob. (*The Flame* 65)

The usage of the blanket term "the leader" not relating to a political, a religious or an administrative leader reveals the oneness of the group led by a single head. "All would wait, praying" irrespective of age, caste and creed. How unified they are! The most vigorous form of social interaction, conflict has umpteen negative effects. Those that are relevant to the study of the poem are dealt with here. Social thinkers have analysed that it is a costly way of settling disputes.

Gill is also on the same line of thought. In the poem the damage caused to the lives of the people is unimaginable:

A man hung out of a window
blood from his head
dripping. (The Flame 52)

The verbal description of the man hanging from the window and the blood dripping from his head emphasizes the hideousness of the abominable act. Gill's detailed picture of the gruesome incident makes the readers recoil in horror:

There was an arm and a head
and a woman's leg
from the knee down
the rest was buried under the rubble.
A body appeared
to have through
a meat grinder.
There was an open chest cavity
beside a headless torso. (The Flame 53)

Gill's vivid account of the body having gone through a meat grinder, of the "open chest cavity beside a headless torso" and of the man in a sitting position split in half unravels the repugnance of the horrendous incident, making the readers shudder at the very thought of it:

At the back of the building
a body was slumped
in a sitting position
and a man was split in half. (The Flame 53)

They saw babies
shrouded in blood ... (*The Flame* 72)

The ghastly and dreadful sketch of the victims is quite heart-ripping. Besides an illustration of the dead, Gill lists a wide range of materialistic damages too. From parking metres to the crumpled cars each and every object that would have been damaged due to such a bloodcurdling incident are discussed elaborately.

Parking metres rent
metal doors twirled
and the lot strewn
with burnt, mangled chassis,
fenders and hoods.

Cars crumpled, flipped
and went into flames.
Some overturned
and some were covered
with rubble. (*The Flame* 56)

Nothing can replace lives. The loss of lives, property and other materials is indeed colossal. It causes social disorder, chaos and confusion:

Several people spent their nights
in sleeping bags,
on cots or folding chairs
stunned or thinking
how they would cope without a brother
child, wife
or mother. (*The Flame* 83)

Confusion, anger, fear, and shock that would quite unconsciously grip the afflicted and those agonizing thoughts that may shroud individuals during such moments are highlighted in the poem. It is not only the causalities that

Gill chronicles but he also records the psychological impairment:

> *Fearing retribution*
> *several families did not speak*
> *and several more*
> *confused, outraged or shocked* ... (*The Flame* 84)

Volunteers, cops, remote- sensing specialists, engineers, investigators, sergeants, medical team and fire fighters involved in rescue operations "wearing a despairing mantle of confusion"(*The Flame* 79) have to manoeuvre through the "ghastly wreckage". (*The Flame* 64)

Conflict also brings in a lot of psychological and moral damages. Besides the plagued relatives of the dead, the rescue operators too are psychologically affected by the incident. They too undergo the same traumatic experience:

> *While carrying an infant*
> *When a cop paused to breathe*
> *he looked down.*
> *He was standing*
> *on a dead child.* (The Flame 72)

The tribulation endured by the cop and the rescuer is indescribable and unimaginable:

> *A rescuer was frozen*
> *when he saw a truck*
> *like the one his son had.* (The Flame 73)

In general fire fighters are considered to be very strong after all the rigorous training that they undertake before and after recruitment into their service. But, in *The Flame,* along with the volunteers, they too are shaken by the chilling truth:

> *The fire fighters wept*
> *as they lifted weightless bodies*

struggling
to retain composure. (75)

shocked volunteers
witnessed a pyramid of ashes
over the cradles -
a bone-chilling calculation... (The Flame 78)

Such a sight weakens their morale, posing varied questions on the wretchedness of life. Sensing the psychological impact, Gill stresses the need for counselling centres during such shocking and gory moments:

Counseling centres sprang up
with psychologists
pastoral assistance...(The Flame 83)

A study of the disjunctive social processes in *The Flame* very specifically conflict, divulges the characteristics of the corporate conflict in the poem. It also unfolds a positive effect and scores of negative effects of conflict - the blowing up of the Day Care Centre. Regardless of the *only* positive effect the 'we feeling' it is worth pondering that the negative effects are quite excruciatingly painful. If it is assumed that the positive effects of conflict outnumbered the negative effects of it, even then no one should be lured by it. The life of a human being is inestimable and irreplaceable.

Nothing should be wrought staking the lives of individuals. If a conflict in a literary work is so stirring how much more will it be when we come to grip with it in reality? Should innumerable innocents be subjected to such a harrowing experience? Is such a conflict an essential part of the society? Is it indispensable? Can't a society progress without it? Should it not be averted? It certainly should be however beguiling it may be. Gill writes: "I believe that peace is the legitimate child of peaceful means" (*The Flame* 21). Only then a peaceful society built solely on love can prevail. Since all human beings aspire for peace, let a world of peace be established.

References

Biesanz, John and Mavis Biesanz. *Introduction to Sociology.* Madras: South Asian Books, 1969.

Gill, Stephen, *The Flame,* Canada: Vesta Publications, 2008.

Green, Arnold W. *Sociology an Analysis of life in Modern Society.* London: McGraw Hill Book Company, 1964.

Rao, Shankar, C.N. *Sociology,* New Delhi: S. Chand & Company, 1994.

Ruhela, Satya Pal, *Introduction to Sociology.* Gurgaon: Shubhi Publications, 2005.

Social Contact, Wikipedia The Free Encyclopedia, 17 Aug. 2008 <en.wikipedia.org/wiki/**Social_contact**>

Social Action. Wikipedia The Free Encyclopedia. 17 Aug. 2008 <en.wikipedia.org/wiki/**Social_action**>

What is Communication? 17 Aug. 2008 <www.natcom.org/nca/admin/index.asp?downloadid =157>

4

A Note on Poetic Craftsmanship in the Prefaces of Stephen Gill

Kalpna Rajput

Stephen Gill, the globally recognized poet, novelist and critic, is also the poet of harmony and recreation of human feelings in the dead veins of humanity. His concern for the world, its people and their values and conscience is the diadem of success on him. His literary career is already studded with several recognitions, awards and honours and his deep concern for the people around is visible in his poetry. Actually the literary oeuvres of the poets mirror their literary bent of mind and it is also indisputably true that 'with this key poets unlock their heart and soul' to their readers. The poetry of Stephen Gill is no exception to this statement.

The prefaces of the books and especially of the books of poetry usually give a graphic glance in the psyche of a poet and have some instances or notes on writings an ideal poetry. Like Dryden or T.S. Eliot, Stephen Gill's criticism is chiefly in the form of prefaces where he both justifies his own poetic creations and propounds certain rules and regulations of writing ideal poetry. He is one of those chosen few poets of the world who besides, providing *spiritual solace* and *intellectual pabulum,* gives invaluable notes (both subjective and objective) on poetry and poetic craftsmanship. This paper focuses on the prefaces of Stephen Gill's major works titled *Shrine* (revised edn.), *Songs Before Shrine*, *Flashes* and *The Flame* wherein the poet has explored some unknown and untouched regions of poetry and its art and craft. Stephen Gill's mind is prone to writing of poetry since his childhood days so his sense of understanding poetry and its principals is much more mature than other poets. George Hines says:

> *He aspired to be a writer from his childhood... He used to write poetry also, which he never bothered to have published because he was never satisfied with his attempts.. Yet he was considered as a poet by his friends. (Stephen Gill and His Works* XXIV)

Stephen Gill considers poetry as the power to relieve the monotonousness of isolation and in more comprehensive term a way to be a mature poet. To him, poetry is a companion to cheer up while dolorousness pervades all-round. The poet, in his early life during his studies in India, found life of the people around him struggling under the trauma of Hindu-Muslim religious fanaticism, so poetry proved to be giving him consoling effects at that time. He himself says:

> *I saw the glass of peace being smashed into pieces when I was growing up in India. I developed the feeling of isolation, rootlessness and terror. The muscles of those feelings smashed the glass of my peace even during the early years of my life. (SBS Preface VIII)*

These quite contradictory situations brought him to the world of poetry. He says:

> *Lack of security in the land of those physicians led me to isolation in the early days that revealed to me the path of my poetic destination. I began to find ways to establish myself as a writer and poet. My struggle was based more on perspiration than inspiration. One can say that it was my inspiration that led me to perspiration. The shadows of inspiration and perspiration walked side by side with me everywhere. I grabbed every opportunity to sharpen my tools to be a better poet. (The Flame* 14-15)

In his prefaces, Stephen Gill has raised two major points particularly, One – *what is poetry?* And the other – *What kind of the poetry must be?* Subsequently, he has also raised the limitations in poetry which to some extent let some fragments of expression remain intact from expressing them in poetic form. In this paper, the discussion will be on these three aspects of poetry focused by Stephen Gill in his prefaces. Gill informs that poetry is not different from life and has an active involvement with its time and its concerns. Poetry, according to him, is the simplified version of complex situations. It is a medium between the poet's self and his surrounding milieu. In the preface of *The Flame* he states:

> *Poetry is an unusual experience that shakes a poet thoroughly. A poem is by a human for human about a deep inner experience that is symbolized through a language. To describe or illustrate, poets need tools and the struggle to master the use of the tools is perspiration. Through images and arrangement of words and other tools, poets convey their experiences to their readers. (The Flame 18)*

Although, experience and inspiration are the basis of penning poetry, the poet also holds perspiration more significant in the process of composing poems O.P. Bhatnagar also supports labour in poetry and observes in the same manner:

> *Poetry is not magic the maneuverings of which can be acquired by smart tricks. It has to be worked on and work after, the labour of which is a virtue and fitness denied to saints and Gods. Sweating makes poetry more organic and less abstract and obtuse. For labour is the poetry of existence.* (*Vision and Voice* 4).

The concept of beauty in poetry has far-reaching effects. Gill considers language, words and images as enhancement to the beauty in poetry. Actually the poetic craftsmanship is a key of poetic beauty. The example of God is nicely hinted by the poet. According to him good poetry is an intellectual exercise dipped in amazing words. So the concept of beauty in poetry is well described by Stephen Gill:

> *I believe there is beauty everywhere. That is what the Bible says in its story on the origin of the universe. After every creation, God said beautiful. There is beauty in every object and so is poetry. Beauty is poetry.* (*The Flame* 17)

His insistence on beauty in poetry can be sought out easily in each of his talk on poetry. He says:

> *Poetry is not only to convey that experience to readers, it is also to convey it in a beautiful way and that beautiful way should also be something like a new and delicious dish. (The Flame* 18)

The very striking point that the poet raises, whether the powerful thoughts suddenly strike a poet's head and heart or he has to do a lot of brain jostling exercise for it. In its answer we may quote his words:

> *There is a myth that poetry strikes a poet like a flash, or it is a divine bolt. For a serious poet, it may be bolt and divine, but mostly it is cooking. (The Flame* 17)

Really, the divine bolt is a rare case for rare geniuses who always submerge themselves in the world of poetry, but in the case of common poets, thoughts do not come naturally to them. They have to commence on the path of mental labour. Famous critic Longinus in *On The Sublime* considers firstly natural thoughts which are coming naturally to a poet and secondly beautiful words, imagery and so forth. But those divine bolts can be used as they are, creating a sweep in the poem and the excess of beautiful words, imagery, symbols, and difficult words create ostentation in an otherwise beautiful poem. So, giving a turn to the subject of creation of a fine verse, Gill tries to judge a poet's work by the ideal truth and power, the perfection and beauty of his presentation and utterance of it. Nevertheless, poetry is a cosmic awareness out of which a poet can have the experiences, the universal beauty and consciousness to human psyche. It exhibits the growth of man's psychological motive and power in words and ideas that form the aesthetic expression of his soul and mind. Gill also says:

> *It is a poet who gives that god a shape with the beauty of the language. Language is a media between an object and poet that gives life, as God did when he created the universe with his words. What is important in a poem is the arrangement of words. This is an intellectual exercise that needs dipping into the amazing world of words. These efforts need the proper knowledge of the tools.* (*The Flame* 18)

In his preface to *Songs before Shrine,* he states on the impact of experience on the poetic tools of an artist and, hard work as an inventory of the good poetry.

> *The tools of an artist keep changing while zigzagging down a labyrinth of experiences. When it is said that artists are born with talent, this implies to me that they have a natural aptitude for particular skills. These aptitudes or talents are rough diamonds to be chiseled and polished to become hard, bright, precious and flawless gems. Writing is a profession and the skill of every profession needs to be improved with hard work, patience and study.* (*SBS* VIII)

Again, the illustration of God is noticeable:

> *Artists strive to touch the highest pinnacle of perfection, but perfection is confined to the divine being who is the creator of the inheritors of his spark of creativity. Prominence is the result of years of labour in obscurity to find a market and an audience.* (*Ibid.*)

God is the eternal spirit of beauty and delight, so also is a poet who takes out the expressive raptures and high revelation of human psyche out of chaos and obscurity. The poet who creates is not only a maker of beautiful words and phrases, but also a spokesman of eternal spirit of beauty and delight.

For Gill, thoughts are the 'airy beings the robins of' his art. 'These robins are not meant to be caged. They are the words of freedom. They enjoy their freedom when poets send them to publications or present them in a book for the enjoyment of the reader.' He says:

> *Poets are wordsmiths who have knowledge and education about the tools that are used to cloth these airy beings in a graceful way. This is an art. A person may be born with a propensity to be a poet, but that is not enough. Propensity and talent is like a raw diamond that has to be chiseled and polished into a beautiful form. In order to acquire the knowledge of chiseling and polishing a poet needs work that I call perspiration. To me poetry is seventy-five percent perspiration and twenty-five per cent inspiration or talent.* (*Kafla Inter-continental* 48)

To enhance the creativity in him, man must realize that he is the child of God, an apex creator of this vast universe. Words are the roads to expression. They are the energy providing device for poems. Stephen Gill says:

> *Poets use words as rocks. History has proved it over and over again that words are the atoms of the nitroglycerin which are suffused with energy. The first poet was God who created the universe with His words. God created human in His own image. In other words, human is also creative.* (*SBS* XX)

Words in poetry have the integral position. They sometimes assume the place of colours and sometimes of lyrics. A person of any stream can see the effect of words in each line of poetry. Sometimes, words become more than a word and become thought content as crucial to poetry. He is well aware of the multi-layered and multi-dimensional nature of poetry and poetic process. So, Stephen Gill thinks that success of a poet depends to a large extent upon the right choice of words.

Poets have great love for words which they nourish with tenderness and give them unique personality. Words in poetry carry fine meaning and gather depth from a fix order of uncertainty enshrined in them which is the outcome of imaginative functioning of human intellect. Whenever a poet fails, it is due to ineffectual use of words. Poetry grows up with words with visionary values. Gill sees the importance of words in poetry from different angle and says:

> *Poets are painters who use words, instead of colours, or they are dancers, who use lyrics instead of using the movements of their hands, legs and facial expressions. In addition to the arrangement of words, the most important in a poem is economy of expression.* (*The Flame* 18)

In the last line, the poet simply suggests that the poet should use words verifying his intent in the poem avoiding the repetitiveness of the same expression with the help of different words. Emotional depth is considered as the hallmark of good poetry. According to him, the poem written with intensity of emotions always stumbles on the stones of typical or unnecessary words. So he says:

> *I believe that the language of poetry is more compact, energetic, of great intensity and emotional depth than the language of prose is, and it has no room for clichés and unnecessary words. Poetry is a villa of glorious shape where every brick that is chiseled in a unique way belongs to its exact spot.* (*SBS* 7)

Poetry is a bridge from internal world to external one. The poet reflects on the world around him and registers his thoughts. The tools of poetry make the poet's ideas more compact and intellectual. Mental and intellectual labour make the poetry devoid of general lacks. In an interview to N. K. Agarwal, Gill discuses these tools and says:

> *I try to use fresh language and images, cautions to use allusions that are hackneyed. Trite expressions are often used in Indian English literature, such as Ram Rajya, apple's eyes, at a stone throw, a faithful friend, Mother nature, leave no stone unturned, wear and tear, axe to grind, nip in the bud and many more. These are worn out phrases. Sometimes, original expressions may be obscure to the reader and may prove enigmatic.* (*Kafla Inter-continental* 49)

For him, while composing poem, language and expression are worth noticing. The poet reflects his soul's self, felt and experienced and its reaction to the objects of external world.

To express something in sensible way, a poet needs intellectual element that is the foundation of poetry. He emphasizes to include intellect in poetry to make people 'think and envision things' afresh and alive. He is of the view that all that guides the poet is the intellectual aspect—the involvement with issues, values and morals in life. He says:

> *Poetry is an art of expression and expression differs as does the appearance of individuals. When a person perceives an object - beautiful or ugly – it produces a reaction or feelings. Those feelings, reactions or sentiments, are formless. A poet expresses those formless objects in a sensible form. One can use a cliché that is easy and needs no effect, but there is no inventiveness in its use. One can find new ways and modes to express the object. That needs real effort. This is called individual approach– a distinctive element– fresh memorable piece of art. Such a treatment needs intellectual exercise. (Ibid* 49-50)

Besides giving his own concept of poetry in his prefaces, Stephen Gill also mentions the shortcomings prevalent in modern poetry. New poets are just writing their thoughts without measuring their adaptability to the basic principles of poetry.

His own approach to poetry is not of enjoying his ideas and considering it as *art for art's* sake but poetry has a motto behind it. He is the harbinger of peace, hope and harmony. He has seen a lot of violence, destruction and terrorism. So, he says:

> *Poetry is to present my vision and my concerns and to conceive peace in a peaceful way. The compelling influence for my crusade is the peace that is beauty, the peace that is creative; the peace that makes life meaningful. I attempt to illustrate that peace in its myriads forms on the rocks of my words. These rocks shout that Lazarus buried under them longs for life.* (*SBS* XXI)

The inquiring eye of Stephen Gill brings forth some limitations in poetry which are frequently found as patches in an otherwise good poetry. These limitations find more space when one tries to compose a long poem that requires the limited range of words, images, thoughts, symbols and expressions. He states:

> *One problem that a poet usually encounters in a long poem is the possibility of repetition of words and phrases. Another is maintenance of logical flow and continuity. I am a proverbial enemy of clichés though some are animating and some may creep in without my being aware of them. I believe that poet should use fresh images. I have tried to use every word carefully as a brick to build the edifice..."* (*The Flame* 9)

So, the shortcomings in modern poetry are:

- *Repetition of words and phrases.*
- *Lack of the maintenance of logical flow and continuity.*
- *Use of clichés.*
- *Lack of fresh images.*
- *Lack of revisions.*
- *Lack of special knowledge to use tools of poetry.*

He feels that often poets do not review their own creations because it is trying calling and needs an observant eye. He says:

> *A poet should never be tired of revisions. A time comes when a poem would tell when to stop. Sometimes poets have to stop revision because they get tired of what leads them nowhere, even knowing that the poem needs extra work. In such situations, I put my poem aside to take it up some other day unexpectedly. This procedure works in most cases with most poets. Often poets will know themselves if a poem needs further work. It is like knowing when the stomach is full. (The Flame* 17)

He also suggests that in case of non-satisfaction one can

'consult an editor' also. Besides, suggesting the techniques and modes of doing good poetry, he also shares his own experiences in this field with his readers with complete honesty. There is clarity and transparency in his self-developed theory of poetry. He accepts that besides inspiration, all labour depends on the poet and says:

> *I began to find ways to establish myself as a writer and poet. My struggle was based more on perspiration than inspiration. One can say that it was my inspiration thul led me to perspiration. The shadows of inspiration and perspiration walked side by side with me everywhere. I grabbed every opportunity to sharpen my tools to be a better poet.* (*The Flame* 14-15)

According to him, the rules of poetry are to be strictly followed. These rules must not be sacrificed on the altar of propagation of poet's views. Views are the soul of poetry but they must be expressed in a suitable form to express the inner- self of the poet. If this process is done successfully, it can be called spiritual liberation unmistakingly. So, he says:

> *Poetry is an art. I do not try to break rules of the art for the sake of the propagation of my views. I am a votary of beauty and beauty is peace. I use poetry also to escape. I feel relieved when I clean the glasses of the self to glimpse a panoramic view of a new Island. I am at my best when my fingers tingle and arms begin to cry. That is the time when I feel happy that I am able to communicate better with the inner self and give birth to my thoughts and feelings. I call this process a type of spiritual liberation.* (*SBS* XXI)

He feels that the mode of expression varies from man to man because every one sees and reacts to a thing according to his nature and 'in a sensible form'. Each creative mind has its own individual approach. Perhaps this is the reason that so many new forms of poetry have been in vogue i.e. Tanka, Haiku, Quatrains and Rondel.

Stephen Gill has always tried to explore something new in the field of poetry. His poetry collection *Flashes* is a 'trilliums in Haiku spirit'. He has well narrated its traditional form and the short history of Haiku. According to him, 'the ignorance of the original shape of Haiku helps to develop its variety.' The history of Haiku in Japan is also that of the constant changes. He favours change in Haiku's traditional form:

> *Most creative artists are not satisfied adhering to established norms, because they want their work to be more unique and personal. This applies to Haiku writers as well. Yet, I am not against established norms as long as they serve some useful purpose. Otherwise, it would become boring to follow the pointless practice of travelling again and again along the same beaten path. It is like trying to fly in a cage. (Flashes* 8)

And he suggests the poets interested in Haiku with proper examples to accept any change in its form 'with open arms' and says:

> *We know stagnant waters become breeding grounds for mosquitoes – anything that becomes stale will soon start to stink. It is in the interest of its health to let Haiku breath in fresh air. No one should be afraid of change or experimentation. If Haiku is alive today, it is largely due to its flexibility to allow new trends to be incorporated into it.* (*Ibid*)

He also advises the poets that they should not 'repeat one element again and again without any purpose' because it 'makes the writing dull'. Secondly, they should use telegraphic language because 'brevity is the soul of poetry' but they should not use it without any reason. He also feels some relaxation in the process of composing Haiku.

He feels that 'there is no need to revise again and again to get rid of articles and verbs without any purpose'. Because of the absence of articles and verbs the meaning is always somewhat confusing that takes away the beauty from poetry.

A poet is actually a medium between his self and his surroundings. It is an inner and tangible conversation so it has always an appeal that creates a magnetic effect in it. It is open and artistically secular and expressive of all forms of human expression. The poor quality of creativity in poetry also arises out of the insensitivity of the poet to the time and surroundings. He says:

> *A poet has to manage an unmanageable horse of emotions that needs skills, guidance and control to be able to achieve smooth efficient operation of a poem. In order to achieve this object, a poet needs time to work in different ways to bring those feelings out... it demands devotion, skill and professionalism.* (*Kafla Inter-Continental* 50)

His idea of poetry is significantly different from that of the other contemporary poets in English. He plans his poems on the basis of idea that appeal to him from time to time. It is a self conscious craft emerging from long contemplation.

For him, poetry is a fortress in which he can roam and strengthen himself with complete sacredness. By giving illustrations from his personal life, he makes the poets realize that poetry can expel the darkness from human life that prick and coax them each time. He summarizes the whole sacred motto of poetry and says:

> *I breathe in the fortress of poetry under the roof of security. Within its genial walls I strengthen the feathers of my pen around the fire of beauty while the demons of daily life surround its entrance of sacredness. I have stopped drinking because of my muse. I have learnt to co-exist with the pangs of the invisible enemies of tension. Nightmares still bother me but poetry opens a gate to calmness from the neurotic world that is full of theatrical despair. Poetry opens a window to breathe the mystical power of catharsis that purifies my emotions about the mirage of the images of my early life. (SBS* XXI)

Thus, the prefaces of Stephen Gill speak volumes of the art and poetic-craftsmanship, definition of poetry, its prevalent limitations and consequent suggestions. Intellectual element is also highlighted in poetry. He doesn't feel that poets are different from common man. They are also 'anxious to share their experiences in order to forge a line of communication that enhances their pleasure'. Stephen Gill also emphasizes the poets to publish their work. The poetry which leads to no expansion of vision frustrates the functions of both mind and poetry.

Each tool of the poetry must be used in balance to make it better. If a good poem is created, it makes the poet feel the paradise, so, he says in his poem 'The World of Poetry':

The world of poetry
Is woven with rainbow strings
Stored in the secret caves of desires
To recreate
The source of that supreme grace
That evolves
In the womb of solitary hours
During the creative nights of its conception. (SBS 40)

References

Baghmar, Dr. G.P. (ed.) *The Vision and Voice, 4,* Nagpur: Vishwa Bharti Prakashan, 1987.

Hines, Dr. George. *Stephen Gill and His Works,* New Delhi: Authors Press, 2008.

Gill, Stephen. *Songs Before Shrine,* New Delhi: Authors Press, 2007. (Abbreviated as *SBS* in the text.)

—. *Flashes,* New Delhi: Imprint, 2007.

—. *Flame,* Canada: Vesta Publications, 2008.

Kafla Inter-Continental, No 36, IICA, Dev Bhardwaj (ed.) Chandigarh. Jan-April 2008, 'Stephen Gill on his Writings and Diaspora' an interview with Dr. N. K. Agarwal.

5

Provenances and Proclamations in Stephen Gill's *Songs Before Shrine*

R. Anandam and G. Baskaran

Every work of art carries the burden of nation, melancholy of citizens, history of places and promises for future. Moreover, it offers a healthy outlet for poet's voice. A harmonious blend of personal and impersonal sources is essential for the production of a good art. Stephen Gill, a poet of diaspora, faces conflicts internally in a comfortable zone. A sense of displacement, dream for peaceful co-existence, aspiration for proclamation, anger against weapon race, admiration for the multi-cultured and tolerant climate, cry for politics, propaganda for universal brotherhood, concern for environment, and minority grievances form the nuclei of his anthology of poems *Songs Before Shrine.* This article attempts to catch those moments which are encounters for any immigrant.

The poem "To Mother" is packed with poet Stephen Gill's sense of guilt and nostalgia for mother's love. Religious intolerance and communal riots forced Gill to seek safer country to live in. He moved to Ethiopia to take teaching profession. But, his interest for writing forced him to settle in Canada. He lived comparatively a peaceful life in both the countries. Canada offered a perfect platform to experiment and master his poetic skills. Still, the poet is haunted by past life in India with a deep sense of remorse. He thinks of his dead mother and his native land which he has left behind for personal reasons. His sense of loss - of both his native land and his mother - is well-portrayed.

In his preface to *Songs Before Shrine*, the poet recollects his last moments with his mother. When the poet informed the mother of his decision to leave India, she did not stand in his way. But, she added that she would not see him again. Her eyes twinkled with a message, meaningful and sad. Her face beaten with age, industry and anxiety remained frozen in the memory of the poet. The poet writes:

Years have gone by
still
I see your tearful eyes. ("To Mother")

Outwardly, the poet appeared calm. But, inwardly he was restless, lacked concentration and took to drinking. Dreams of communal violence in India made him sick. Mother used to appear in his dreams to reassure his mental balance. The poet observes:

Your name emanates
in pleasing designs. ("To Mother")

Gill portrays his mother as image of Sacrifice and message of Hope. He fondly dedicates his lucrative life to her. Readers are moved to tears when Gill expresses his desire in the following lines:

Mother dear
I wish you were here. ("To Mother")

Dove as a symbol of world peace is handled effectively by the poet in his poem "Seeking the Dove of Peace". Gill expects his readers to join him in the effort to bring peace to the world. At the same time, the poet records with displeasure that peace as a phenomenon has ever been an eluding factor 'since Adam's time'. But, his search is relentless. The poet seeks the bird everywhere 'above the snow-capped hills / into the bewildered valleys'.

In his attempt to bring back the bird, Gill goes to the extent of enquiring even the beasts. The poet could faintly hear its melody, see its face, feel the beat, envision its flight, and smell its presence. In the last stanza, he tries to emphasize the idea of universal brotherhood and the need for solidarity. Citizen of the world must stand united 'like brothers' and work together for the cause of peace. The poet acknowledges their helplessness yet calls them not to abandon their effort in the following lines:

Though blind-folded
yet bound in a design
let us go. ("Seeking the Dove of Peace")

Towards the end of the poem, he infuses a sense of urgency in the readers' mind to search and find the dove of peace. The world with all its diversity and richness is a Heaven. Peace is the basic element which sustains its existence. If peace is displaced by lawlessness, human beings are deprived of their right to live in this world. The poet calls for a collective effort to restore peace all over the world before it is too late. He concludes the poem with these lines:

Directing one another
let us march
to embrace that dove
before we die. ("Seeking the Dove of Peace")

In his short poem "To Be", Gill tries to explain the power of poetry and the reason why he wants to be a poet. The poetic muse converts the writer's pen into a plough to sow the seeds of peace in his land. The ferocious tongues of the ongoing violence 'fan the smoulders' of the poetic spirit 'into the burning flames.' The blaze will consume 'all that is gross' in his writing. His poetry thus emerges as a gold and shine eternally for peace.

The poet wants to produce a number of great poems to enlighten people.

I wish to harvest
a ripened manna of wonders
of the youthful bloom
for the court of enlightenment. ("To Be")

Gill wants to validate the claim that diversity as a concept has its roots in the cosmic world. The spring season, empowered by the poet's lyrics, dances to the song of life. Gill believes that his poetry has got strength to infuse life and enlightenment in people. He thinks that even nature would respond positively to his lyrics. So, the poet writes with a sense of confidence:

Fragrance of spring
sustain a structure of strength
with the braces of my lyrics. ("To Be")

The poem "When" traces the evolution of universe and the origin of human beings which is contrasted with destruction and road to disaster. According to Big Bang theory, the universe was created from quark, a group of subatomic particles believed to form protons, neutrons, etc. When the quark expanded, there was fusion between the atomic particles to form galaxies. In total, 10 galaxies form the universe. Thus, the universe evolved with atomic particles fusing one another. This fusion is the result of attraction between the particles to form several elements. This implies a cordial relation between particles, which resulted in creation. Gill wants to emphasize his idea that mutual acceptance for variation would allow for evolution of new order. He says:

When
harmony was established
among the stars, sun, moon and earth
and every other object
the universe was carved. ("When")

The second stanza of the poem "When" traces the origin of human being in the world. According to the Bible, Adam and Eve reconciled God's ways and paved the way for proliferation of mankind. Darwin's theory on evolution of species undermines mutual agreement between life forms which facilitated the origin of humankind.

When
harmony was fused
into the mind, soul, heart
and every other organ of the body,
the human was created. ("When")

The third stanza portrays the origin of peace. Power of reason enabled human being to understand natural forces, domesticate wild animals and cultivate lands. Thus, mankind could establish harmony with external world to bring peace in life. The poet says:

When
harmony symphonizes
nature, humans
and every creature of animal kingdom,
peace emerges. ("When")

The last stanza strikes a warning for the entire world to reflect upon. The two world wars projected a gory picture of devastation. The womb of earth bled with thousand cuts. The nuclear bomb exploded hearts of million. Cold War promoted weapon trade. Mad race for superpower status destabilized Republics. Partition resulted in separation of families. The scars on the face of humanity are so deep and painful that they refuse to heal. The poet aptly recalls the past history of destruction and pain in the following lines:

When
harmony disintegrates
the gates of hell open wide
for lava to flow. ("When")

In the preface, *Journey of Stephen Gill: Autobiographical,* the poet has impressed on the fact that a person is largely the product of the environment. Canada is the best example of co-existence of a society with diverse cultures and faith. It is a country where the Government legally supports multiculturalism to foster tolerance.

Gill cherishes particularly the tolerant attitude of the country to other races and religions. Hence, the poet is full of praise for the country in the poem "My Canada". The country is, according to the poet:

A nation so great
diverse and brave. ("My Canada")

The country is the abode of peace, tolerance and diversity. The conducive ambience that prevails in the country, the sense of security and self esteem enjoyed by the citizens are the product of the deliberate policies adopted by the Government. Canada is one of the most preferred countries for the people who wish to settle abroad. Hence, the poet rightly feels:

Thy soul
a serene temple
for every creed
for every breed. ("My Canada")

In the poem "The Meechlake Fish", Gill personifies terrorism as a crocodile. Often, terrorism assumes sacred titles such as holy war, religious duty, territorial sovereignty, etc. Terrorism is operated under the disguise of politics, religion and race. The crocodile 'with a tail for deliberate ruin' is rightly compared to the Meechlake Fish. In this context, Gill makes an allusion to Canada's first attempt at a major political reform. The Canadian Constitution Act (1982) allowed making changes to the governing framework. Quebec had its own reservations. An accord was signed at a resort called Meech Lake. Canada was badly divided over this amendment. The accord poised to develop territorial division of the country. Many Canadians believed that Canada as a nation might break apart as it failed to recognize the unique status of the aboriginal people. Gill criticizes the accord as 'a crocodile of racial disharmony'. It disturbed the 'crystal flow' of life in the country. People who are afraid of racial discrimination 'seek softer spots'. The writer, for instance, abandoned his home soil due to horrors of Partition and communal riots in India.

The poet is angry at politicians who divide people on imaginary lines. Canada is an example for ideal country. Life in Canada moves smoothly. But the poet could spot autumn lurking along the banks. Provincial unrest will certainly divide the country and debase the name. So, the poet asks a valid question: *Why does autumn lurk on the banks?*

The poem concludes with another question to ponder about. Solutions for issues can be achieved through bilateral discussions. Successful negotiation should be balanced and realistic with mutual respect for both sides. Agreements will yield desired result if only people practise habits of tolerance and acceptance. But, in reality, discussion as a source for solving disputes is restored at last. Accords and agreements are always self-centered. People practise discrimination without sympathy. This state of affairs allows the crocodile of disharmony to lay and hatch their eggs. The poet wonders:

And why is there more excavation
for the hard-shelled eggs
of the crocodiles? ("The Meechlake Fish")

The poem "Unfair Ophelia" is the poets' brooding over his poetic career. Adopting the eternal lines from Shakespeare's masterpiece, *Hamlet* (Act III, Scene I), Gill indulges in contemplation regarding the purpose of his poetry. Hamlet, in the play, suffers mental agony due to crisis at all levels, domestic, personal, and political. Similarly, the poet devastated by religious bigotry, insecurity, past memories, and anxiety to find his feet in the creative world involves in deep unreconciled contemplation.

Should writers resign themselves
to the stench of your structure
of injustice
braced by the barbs of bigotry
or uncover your ugliness
at the shrine of law and liberty? ("Unfair Ophelia")

Shakespeare's Ophelia is a sweet, innocent maid, meek, and submissive to elderly authority. She allows herself to become a helpless tool in the complications of the story. Likewise, violence in the hands of politicians like Laertes, Claudius and Polonius serves as a helpless puppet. The poet personifies it as a woman who dances to their delight and plays an unfair game. Violence is an endless road which takes travellers nowhere. So, the author finds violence, personified as woman who is lacking in independent spirit, to play a fair game. The main problem with the poet is whether he should go on writing poems uncovering human high-handedness or resign himself, which will be suicidal. Which is nobler in spirit? Is it worthy trying hard to produce a piece of art for self-appeasement? Or is it better to kill past memories in the poetic domain? Through his lament, Gill also proposes his theory on art of writing poetry. He, in his preface, "Me and My Poetry" states that poetry is a villa of glorious shape where every brick that is chiselled in a unique way belongs to its exact spot.

Like other arts, poetry needs revision for perfection. Artists strive to touch the highest pinnacle of perfection, but perfection is confined to Divine Being who created the inheritors of His spark. Hence, the poet writes:

Writers must use their coin
that is the Lord's wish. ("Unfair Ophelia")

But, racial winds blow strong enough to deflower the poets' hope for the better world. Can poets afford to reconcile the scorn and humiliation over minorities? Can poets turn deaf ears to the wrong and injustice inflicted upon minorities? These questions confront Gill to the point of madness.

Should poets
let the flower of hope be wasted
by the sickles of racial winds
is the question now. ("Unfair Ophelia")

Violence bloom and flourish at the expense of public properties, loss of lives and brain drain. Communal disharmony and intolerance make most intellectuals restless who become incapable of productive action. So, they abandon their soil and seek refuge on the lap of their chosen land. This is a national loss, according to the poet. Demolition, Immolation and Humiliation are pointers to lunaticism. Such incidents project a dreary and ugly picture of the nation to the world. So, the poet chides at the various forms of human rights violation in a flat tone: *You debase the name of the nation.*

From time immemorial, politicians thoughtlessly use military power as a mean to settle political issues. The two world wars promoted enmity among nations and degraded human values. Thus, war proved to be an ineffective tool to bring peace in the world.

The seeds of enmity have fostered hatred and intolerance. The seeds have grown as a deep forest, which does not allow light to enter. Hence, it is always dark and there is no way out. It engulfs all who enters the land. The poet warns the irrevocable nature of terror as follows:

Be soft
unfair Ophelia
fear the fire of that undiscovered land
from which no traveller has returned. ("Unfair Ophelia")

The last stanza summarily projects his conviction. Ordinary people may remain indifferent and inert to the horrors, both modern and primitive. But, creative writers always look at the odd corner to unravel the eerie nature of elements. It is their moral obligation to write on such subjects to serve the society in their own way.

The poet's monologue serves as a vehicle of thought to illustrate his poetic theory, his aversion for atrocities and determination to create work of art. Gill's "A Question" is a direct attack on the mad race for nuclear supremacy. The nations that are armed with nuclear capabilities are lurking dangers to world peace. The poet raises a volley of question and tries to evoke response from readers. The poem begins with these lines:

If the nuclear bombs drop
Will the buds bloom again?
Will the birds chirp again?
Will the spring return again? ("A Question")

The ultimate victim of a possible nuclear holocaust will be the Nature. But, when nature takes its course of action, it is merciless. Nature appears to be resilient to abuse of all kinds. But, as science reports, the planet earth is still an active element with lava red hot at its core. Advocates of science compare the surface of the earth to the thickness of apple's skin. The poet registers his concern for environment when he asks:

Will rains kiss the earth again?
....
Will the dawn be born again? ("A Question")

It is a popular opinion that if third world war breaks, the world will be reduced to ashes. According to the Bible, Noah's ark came to the rescue when the world was destroyed by the deluge. But, man made vessels are too fragile and incompetent that no one can escape the wrath of nature. Even the Almighty will hesitate to spare any life on earth as man has broken the divine link. So, the poet concludes the poem with a shocking interrogation: *Will God save anyone?*

The ultimate objective of the poet, in writing poetry is to assert universal brotherhood. But many barriers stand as goliath in the name of religion, nationality, race, etc. Man is born free but a series of link binds him to confinement. The poet enters into a personal conversation with readers answering basic questions in the poem "I am still a man". The poet follows and respects Christian values just because he was brought up in a Christian family. He was not a Christian by birth. Thus, religion became the first link of his chain of bondage. It is human predicament to accept the religion of parents. But, he never isolated himself from festivals of other religion. In his article, "Me and My Poetry", Gill says: "We participated in the social festivities of the Holi and Diwali of our neighbourhood". The poet's family lived peacefully in Sialkot. The breakup of the country separated his relatives and friends.

Thus, partition played its role to fasten him in the endless chain. These knots are forced and irreversible. But, ironically, Gill disowns religions and nationality in these lines:

My religion
Was not my choice;
Yet I love all creeds ("I am still a man")

According to Hindu mythology, the process of birth is manipulated by Lord Brahma, a three-headed figure. He is the creator of life. If all life originates from Brahma, the poet's life also hails from the same source. In this fashion, Gill a child of the Hindu God, worships Jesus. The poet says:

I am also / Your God's child. ("I am Still a Man")

The poet witnesses horrors of Partition when India was divided. In the article, "Me and My Poetry", the author says: "Partition of India resulted in the death of around two million people and around fourteen million were forced to migrate from one country to another. and about seventeen thousand women were abducted and raped". There was chaos around. In *Journey of Stephen Gill: Autobiographical,* the author says: *"That harsh and unfriendly atmosphere has shaped a global outlook in me".* So he says:

I am a human
I love humankind
smile, my friend
because
we are all one. ("I am Still a Man")

The poet will be satisfied, at least if the people of India and Pakistan join together again. Like the poet's chosen country, the two countries if united will emerge as a safer spot. Minority people live a pathetic, insecure life and are always looked as an outsider. In some cases, they are subjected to forceful conversion. In certain cases, they are threatened to migrate. These people undergo ingenious, illogical trails and tribulations to prove their innocence without any fault of their own. They are forced to live a miserable life in Government run relief camps with less food and little sanitation. They are objects of abuse and neglect by the majority. Gill offers prayer to God to protect these ill-fated people in "These Children".

It is to be acknowledged that minority people participate in the development of nation. They form the crux of multi-culture. In the article, *Journey of Stephen Gill: Autobiographical,* the author states that happy minorities will contribute towards nation building. If minorities feel secure, they will do everything to feel proud of their heritage. It is fun to have flowers and fruits of different shades and kinds in the same orchard. Uniformity and homogeneity in the political and religious climate is a utopian thought.

Gill fervently prays to God to allow these people to flourish. In his prayer, he sends a piece of message that it is the duty of the Government to extend a moral support to minorities so that they may add infinite varieties to the native culture. The poet writes:

> *Gardener*
> *nurture the growth of these roots*
> *with rare delicacies of concerns.* ("These Children")

According to the poet, the talents, knowledge and skills of minority people need to be identified which could be utilized for building the strength of the nation. Given the opportunities, they would prove a critical team to elevate the position of the country to the next level. The poet believes that minorities have much in store and they are unharnessed. A flock of people from this neglected section of society have already enriched and projected the image of the country, India.

Former President of Indian Republic, A.P.J. Abdul Kalam, for instance, contributed his mettle in the defence of the nation and occupied a permanent place in the hearts of Indians. He hailed from a minority community. So, the poet appeals to the Government of world nations to give them due care in these lines:

> *The voyage*
> *of the meaningful explorations*
> *for the innerself*
> *they have yet to embark.* ("These Children")

Gill's rich experience at two different nations and their respective cultures and environments contribute enormously to the anthology, varying from violence to relationships. The poet's attempt for tracing peace and his discomfort over its search are vividly presented in the poems chosen for study. He has also given a chance of experiencing both the Partition moments and post independence fragrance in his poems.

References

www.stephengill.ca

Gill, Stephen. *Me and My Poetry.*

—. *Journey of Stephen Gill: Autobiographical*

6

The Prophet and *The Flame*: A Comparative Study

Sudhir K Arora

He is an angel, sent by the goddess to
Preach the Deity's gospel;
he is a brilliant lamp, unconquered by darkness
And inextinguishable by the wind. It is filled with
Oil by Ishtar of Love, and lighted by Apollon of Music

(*Khalil Gibran Reader* 321)

What Khalil Gibran said about the poet applies not only to himself but also to Stephen Gill. Both the poets—Khalil Gibran and Stephen Gill are the brilliant lamps filled with oil by Ishtar of Love and lighted by Apollon of Music. While going through Stephen Gill's *The Flame*, Gibran's *The Prophet* strikes the mind of a reader or critic. It is a natural tendency of a critic to make a comparative study of the text that he studies with the other text that he has already studied because such a study offers him a choice though, sometimes, confuses him as it unearths some points that make him indecisive to the extent that he hesitates in stating any final word about them. But, out of this comparative study, he explores the unexplored spaces with the critical tools—comparison and analysis—which help him in evaluating the texts. "These critical tools attract the critics who use them to justify the points arising somewhere in the mind that provides the unlimited space for the explorations of the critical insight. They, sometimes, help in providing a better perspective for the text that is to be studied and, sometimes, disappoint by offering a weak scenario on being compared.

Hence, there may be a chance for a prejudiced assessment as it is generally believed that a text differs and must differ from the other text and no comparison should be motivated as different texts come from different environment" (*Contemporary Vibes* 52). But, it does not mean the technique of comparison is not worth applying. It opens the fresh portals for the interpretations which are helpful in making an assessment of the text.

Khalil Gibran, who came to be noted as "the Bard of Washington Street", wrote his masterpiece *The Prophet* which took him more than eleven years to write and perfect. *The Prophet* is "widely acclaimed as one of the most spiritual books ever written" (Cover). Besides its spiritual undertones, its twelve illustrations by the author himself add the beauty of the text. Stephen Gill, who is better known as "the Bard of Peace" for promoting the values of tolerance, understanding and co-existence in the world where there will be justice, love, harmony and brotherhood, has penned *The Flame* which is the result of the eight years labour. *The Flame* is heralded as Stephen Gill's masterpiece on terrorism, a contemporary problem which has taken the world in its embrace. It is a long poem about the destruction caused by maniac messiahs. Like *The Prophet,* it has devotional and spiritual touches. Gill has not inserted illustrations like Gibran but he has created the picturesque landscapes through his words. He invokes the Flame, depicts the havoc and destructive scenes, calculates the loss, studies the maniac messiahs psychologically peeping into their hearts and finally offers his stand of pursuing his odyssey. His tone is inbuilt didactic. Gibran's *The Prophet* is didactic as Almitra asks Almustafa for some moral precepts:

> *"Yet this we ask ere you leave us, that you speak to us and give us of your truth. / And we will give it unto our children, and they unto their children, and it shall not perish"* (*The Prophet* 16).

Khalil Gibran's *The Prophet* is teemed with teachings concerned with different aspects of life. Love, marriage, children, work, joy and sorrow, laws, freedom, time, prayer, beauty, religion, etc. are such aspects which are preached by Almustafa before the people of Orphalese. It opens the window for peace which lies in soul and it can be traced through spiritualism. Though Almustafa speaks to the people, he is not sure whether he spoke or listened what was spoken.

"Was it I who spoke? Was I not also a listener?" (*The Prophet* 114) Gill's *The Flame* is also replete with moral and spiritual lessons though implicit in nature. It is clothed in the contemporary realism. Very clearly it reflects the relations of men to men who possess the Flame in them. Gill has employed the pronoun 'You' mostly for the Flame—the eternal flame that knows "no occupation, faith nor complexion and cannot be imprisoned within human bonds" (*The Flame* 28) while Gibran has used 'You' to address the people of Orphalese.

When a priestess asks Almustafa to speak of Prayer, he satisfies her query saying: "You pray in your distress and in your need; would that you might pray also in the fullness of your joy and in your days of abundance. / For what is prayer but the expression of yourself into the living ether? (*The Prophet* 92) Prayer is just the expression of a man's self into the living ether. Gibran thinks that God does not listen to man's words until or unless He himself utters them through man's lips. It is God who utters through the lips of man. Almustafa states: "God listens not to your words save when He Himself utters them through your lips" (*The Prophet* 94). It is He who knows well what a man wants. It is He who knows man's needs before hand. He is man's needs and when he gives more of Himself, He gives His all. Gibran's God is omniscient and also caretaker while Gill's God is omnipresent through *The Flame*. For him, *The Flame* is the manifestation of God. He considers *The Flame* as "the driving force that lifts / spirits from the ditches" (*The Flame* 36). *The Flame* is the creation and its meaning can be sensed only through "the glasses of peace". It is not merely "a notable flavoured path" which begins from home but also "the adoring destiny" (*The Flame* 36) that is being trailed by men. He seems to have complete faith in God through the Flame and considers it nirvana, a stage every man aspires to attain. Hence, both Gibran and Gill have shown their unflinching faith in God who, besides being omniscient and omnipresent, knows what is best for human beings. A question arises: Does God wish destruction? Certainly not. God leaves man free to do work in certain spheres. Gibran does not feel the need of going to temple. For him, daily life is the temple as well as religion. Mark the excerpt: "Your daily life is your temple and your religion. / Whenever you enter into it take with you your all" (*The Prophet* 107).

What a man does daily is not less than his prayer and to perform it in a proper manner is his religion. For Gibran, God is ubiquitous as man can see Him "walking in the cloud, outstretching His arms in the lightning and descending in rain/ ...smiling in flowers, then rising and waving His hands in trees" (*The Prophet* 108) while, for Gill, the Flame is "the quietness over the meadows / where / the lush vegetation sprawl / in the gulf of the spring" (*The Flame* 43).

The poet in Gill is stunned not to find the Flame in his deep meditation and, hence, opens his eyes and stops counting of beads. He feels himself a lamb that needs a good shepherd. He is a seeker who seeks peace not in meditation but in humanity. His soul is bruised when he sees destruction caused by the maniac messiahs. To remove the pain and suffering of the humanity is his pious prayer. He seeks the blessings of the Flame for this work. He prays to the Flame to give him the softness of her light "to weed out the spite / the Dark / the frowning evil / the war / the misery / the hard days / and for dialogue to guide / the good to lead" (*The Flame* 110). Service to humanity is his prayer to the Flame or God.

For Gibran, man cannot direct the course of love but it is love that directs the course of man if it finds him worthy. It never comes out of selfish motive as "Love gives naught but itself and takes naught but from itself" (*The Prophet* 21) and it neither possesses nor is possessed. For him, God is supreme authority and to love Him is the desired goal. He makes man proud of him in declaring that he is in the heart of God rather than God is in his heart. It is love that has "no desire but to fulfill itself" (*The Prophet* 21). For Gill, love is core subject of his poetry. It is the love for God that inspires him to embrace the whole humanity. His love for the Flame i.e. God possesses *sufiana* colour. He praises the Flame for her eyes which seem to be "a seaside retreat / where mystic flames reign / and / nature courts the night's favor / for a feast of peace" (*The Flame* 37). He considers himself as "the restlessness of the cloud" and the Flame as "the lightning of thunder / that kindles / the fires of trust" (*The Flame* 42). Unlike Gibran who believes himself in God, Gill feels God i.e. the Flame in him. Mark the excerpt: "you dwell in the mysteries / of my veins / to sweep away the cobwebs / of despair" (*The Flame* 42). Gibran also believes in the flame and has regards for it. No doubt, wise men come and give moral lesson through wisdom.

He does not believe in wisdom rather he wishes to take wisdom out of man as he has found the thing which is greater than wisdom. It is the flame in spirit. Mark the excerpt when Almustafa speaks to the people of Orphalese: "Wise men have come to you to give you of their wisdom. I came to take of your wisdom: / And behold I have found that which is greater than wisdom. / It is a flame spirit in you ever gathering more of itself, / While you, heedless of its expansion, bewail the withering of your days" (*The Prophet* 122). For Gill, the Flame is everything and without it, he cannot think of his existence. He calls the Flame a balance in creation. It is "the binding force / for families, planets / every atom / and every part of every individual" (*The Flame* 135). To think of life without the Flame is impossible for him. It is he who states: "Life disintegrates / where the rays of flame / do not reach" (*The Flame* 135). On the matter of 'the flame spirit as greater than wisdom', both Gibran and Gill seem to be shaking hands with each other.

Man is himself responsible for good and evil. It is his conscience that makes evil suppress when it tries to get upper hand. If evil gets upper hand crushing conscience, man succumbs to evil. Gibran observes that nothing happens unknowingly rather seeds are already present in man. He illustrates it through the example of leaf and tree. He states: "And as a single leaf turns not yellow but with the silent knowledge of the whole tree, / so the wrong-doer cannot do wrong without the hidden will of you all" (*The Prophet* 60). Gill also thinks in the line of Gibran when he realizes that men are responsible for strengthening the destruction. He agrees to Gibran's excerpt: "And if it is a despot you would dethrone, see first that his throne erected within you is destroyed" (*The Prophet* 69). Maniac messiahs are powerful because of the weaknesses of the masses. They tempt men with "knowledge, / easy money and weight" in order to become their messiahs while in truth they enjoy in stilling "the nightingale of freedoms / uprooting the tree where the bird sings" (*The Flame* 102). They are monsters in the guise of messiahs who are interested only in destruction. Mark the excerpt for their intentions: "They crush buds / with bulldozers / wearing the gown of sanctimony / to cover the nakedness / of their disease / that eats away / the flesh of peace" (*The Flame* 134). These so-called messiahs befool the masses on the name of religion, race and caste.

To make the masses aware of these so-called messiahs through his poetry has become his goal and he will pursue it throughout his life. As he confides in Gibran's excerpt: "Surely there is no greater gift to man than that which turn all his aims into parching lips and all life into a fountain" (*The Prophet* 123), he will pursue his "odyssey through the barren regions of the moor" (*The Flame* 152).

Going through *The Prophet* makes the reader forget his cares. He forgets himself and is lost in the moral precepts of Almustafa and learns the secrets of a good life. He feels joy and sorrow inseparable. Joy is the unmasked sorrows. The line "The deeper that sorrow carves into your being, the more joy you can contain" (*The Prophet* 45) strengthens him enough to tolerate the sorrow. He begins to believe with Almustafa that joy and sorrow come together and "when one sits alone with you at your board, remember that the other is asleep upon your bed" (*The Prophet* 45). Gibran's text is rich in symbols. But, the symbols that he uses are not complex. Mark the excerpt that reveals the secret of a good life through the symbols of flowers and bees:

> *Go to your fields and your gardens, and you shall learn that it is the pleasure of the bee to gather honey of the flower,*
> *But it is also the pleasure of the flower to yield its honey to the bee.*
> *For to the bee a flower is a fountain of life,*
> *And to the flower a bee is a messenger of love,*
> *And to both, bee and flower, the giving and the receiving of pleasure is a need and an ecstasy.*
> *People of Orphalese, be in your pleasures like the flowers and the bees. (The Prophet,* 100-101)

His diction is simple though rich in meanings and interpretations. He is communicative but sometimes his teachings become ambiguous as different interpretations come out of them. For instance:

> *How often have you sailed in my dreams. And now you come in my awakening, which is my deeper dream. (The Prophet* 9)
> *For when my wings were spread in the sun their shadow upon earth was a turtle.*
> *And I the believer was also the doubter; (The Prophet* 126)
> ....
> *And thus your freedom when it loses its fetters becomes itself the fetters of a greater freedom. (The Prophet* 69)

Stephen Gill also sometimes echoes the tone of Gibran. For instance:

A pleasant wind
carries us away
freed from chains
hair rumpled
we are attuned to the stars.
Along the self-composed clouds
we trail. (The Flame 116)

Gibran speaks in a compact and concise way that leads further to other ways. What makes his lines appealing is their soothing effect. They have a rhythm that runs throughout the text making it memorable. Who can forget such lines: "Shall the day of parting be the day of gathering?" (*Prophet* 10), "You give but little when you give of your possession. / It is when you give of yourself that truly give" (*Prophet* 31) and "A little while, a moment of rest upon the wind, and another woman shall bear me" (*Prophet* 133). Gill is not as simple as Gibran is. He is more poetic and picturesque than Gibran. Gibran makes the reader reflect while Gill makes the reader think. Gill has created the illustrations through words. Mark the excerpt for the picturesqueness of his imagery:

My feet rest in the waters
but the mouth is parched.
Near ripples I lie
both solitary sides
stare at the banks tearfully
to kiss each other's dry lips
while the waters flow by. (The Flame 115)

The comparative study between *The Prophet* and *The Flame* reveals similarities and dissimilarities as the two texts are written in different environments. The present dismal scenario has forced Gill to pen against the terrorism, the monster that has swallowed the lives of the countless children, women and men. He talks of the welfare of the masses. His aim is to awaken the people who are being cheated by the maniac messiahs. He makes them think so that they may be united to face the monster. Gibran talks of the secrets that make life meaningful and worth living. His teachings console the people who are inspired and enchanted by the way they are uttered. For him "to love life through labour is to be intimate with life's inmost secret" (*The Prophet* 41).

Gill is optimistic in life and, hence, believes that one day the world will become free from the clutches of terrorism and there will be peace and prosperity all around. This peace will ultimately lead to spiritual peace, the ever desired goal. Mark the excerpt for such affirmative attitude of the poet in Gill who will continue his fight against the destructive forces: "Poetry / has not flown to distant fields. / Snow still falls / outside the window / and the sun melts away / coldness from homes" (*The Flame* 97). Both the poets are quite relevant in their domains. If Khalil Gibran had been alive today, he would have certainly written on terrorism. If Gill had not experienced the pain and misery out of destructive forces, he would have certainly written on the secrets that might open the door to a most successful life that ultimately makes human spiritual. By recommending peace, Gill hints for such a life. Without peace no life can be successful. It is peace which is the fundamental requirement of life in this global era. Both the poets are nightingales that sing the songs to soothe the depressed and oppressed hearts so that they may get encouragement to continue their struggle for peace through labour. The Prophet in Gill speaks about the Flame that restrains inexorable savageries and the prophet in Gibran has traced in man "a flame spirit" that is greater than wisdom. What Gibran writes about the duties and the difficult tasks that a poet has to perform is quite applicable to him and Stephen Gill.

Poet, you will one day rule the hearts, and
Therefore, your kingdom has no ending.
Poet, examine your crown of thorns; you will
Find concealed in it a budding wreath of laurel.

(*Khalil Gibran Reader* 322)

References

Arora, Sudhir K., "Krishna and Candida: A Comparative Study", *Contemporary Vibes*. vol. No.: 4. no. 13 Oct.-Dec. 2008.

Gibran, Khalil, *The Prophet*, New Delhi: Hind Pocket Books Pvt. Ltd., 2002.

Gibran, Khalil, *Khalil Gibran Reader*, Bombay: Jaico, 1981 (second combined Jaico impression).

Gill, Stephen, *The Flame*, Canada: Vesta Publication, 2008.

7

Hope in the Poetry of Stephen Gill

Shaleen Kumar Singh

"Hope" is the thing with feathers-
That perches in the soul-
And sings the tune without the words-
And never stops-at all-" (*Dickinson* 254)

Undoubtedly, 'Hope' is the thing which perches in the soul of poets and usually seen in their outpourings, empowering both the poet and the readers. In fact, 'Hope' has been the last weapon of a poet who loses all courage and zeal in his combat with toils, trails, troubles and tribulations. It is the spring of poets' inspiration that ever infuses vigour and zeal into their veins.

Poets who motivate mankind are always surcharged with the energy of hope and their poetic outpourings remain clad in the garb of new vigour and enthusiasm even in the darkest hour of dejection. To Emily Dickinson, "Hope is the thing with feathers that perches in the soul and sings the tune without the words." To Stephen Gill it is a constant companion on the trail of pains and pleasures and it 'sings lullabies/ in the morning' and welcomes him 'with a flower of dreams.' "The Maid of Hope" remains with the poet day in and day out. He says:

When I collect
the beads of my thoughts
she scatters them
and when I am upset
she shows skies
through the window
of the future. (Shrine 147)

Hope is nothing but the silver lining in the abysmal darkness of uncertainty which drives the poet back on the shore of liveliness and infuses new zeal into him as well as 'emerges /as sun in the void of solitude to dispel 'the birds of depression.' Stephen Gill's poetry, though a protest against the global terrorists, fanatics and the enemies of peace, reaches sometimes the *Nadir* of gloom. Yet it never deviates from its path of delivering a universal message of peace because the poet remains hopeful unto the last. He is well-aware of the thing called hope from the very inception of his life when he 'was growing up in Delhi' in the atmosphere of riots and clashes. Remembering those days, he says:

> *I have experienced their stings. I know what fear is in the jungle of helplessness. I know what hope is when there is no hope. (Flame* 26)

Somewhere else he seems searching hope and finding it in poetry, he says:

> *To find hope I traced, riches, education, faiths and many other things. I tried to see the face of hope in political ideologies, including Marxism, Nazism and Dictatorship...*

And he adds:

> *To take the root of fear out, I took a long and painful journey of efforts. ... Writing particularly poetry is one way to do that. Poetry is my refuge and my helper to help others to be aware of the enemies of peace.* (*Flame* 27)

If we read between the lines, we will find that the poet

traced hope in riches, education and faith but later on found it in the refuge of poetry or say more directly, poetry became the treasure-trove of hope for Stephen Gill. If we look at his poetic canvas objectively, we will find that hope has been cocoon that has woven it very minutely and meticulously.

Dr. George Hines admits the presence of hope in many of Gill's poems. He says:

> *Many poems express frustrations, sorrow, regret and despondency because of the present state of man and the world, but other poems express hope in better future. (SGHW* 90)

The comments of Dr. George Hines are worth quoting again:

> *Although the poet shows keen awareness of man's personal and global problems in his poems of hope, he feels that they will be resolved, that life is always improving and will be better in the future, and that a fresh dawn with an unclouded sky is approaching. (SGHW 91)*

The fascinating and mature talent of Stephen Gill which is marked with optimism, hope, vigour, zeal, enthusiasm, faith, reliance and assurance require comprehensive appraisal so that the future poets and critics may know what poetry is and what poetry should be. The vision of Gill is imbued with the hope for peace, hope for love, hope for harmony and hope for a new and better world where naked dance of maniac messiahs does not torment humanity, 'where waves snuggles sand/ and soul is free, where the horns of life/ are not entangled in the bushes/ of the zealots.../ where the cactus of shame / does not mushroom / and the evils birds of the bloodshed/ do not defile the nest...' where 'the dove flies without fear/ and the lilies of justice blossom for all', where the streams of youth/ do not cease flowing/ and despair does not nail tents /over the greenery of the dreams', 'where love is not suffocated/ and twigs are not damaged/ by the trotting swarm of savages...' and 'where creeds are not crushed/ and human gods do not feed/ the vultures of war...' (*Flame* 146)

His collection *The Flame* is nothing but a realization – conscious or unconscious– that 'hope is still alive under the sun'. The last canto of the book gives plenty of examples of hope after the symbolic story of *Zeus,* a Greek God, who handed over a box 'containing pain, bloodshed, fear, economic strangulation to Pandora with a forbiddance to open it'.

But it was unfortunately opened by her and the contents of the box began to roam in the world. Again one can observe the following comment of Gill when he relates this symbolic story:

> *All that was left was hope. Eventually it was also let out of that box. Expression of hope is in the last canto of The Flame.* (*Flame* 24)

The Flame is the *magnum opus* of peace. Although, it is the longest poem in English on modern terrorism, it is the most potent and sacred poetic offering to goddess of peace. The book mirrors the naked dance of maniac messiahs and also shows how these openers of the Pandora's Box roam in the world in every shape to cause as much destruction as possible. He adds:

> *They go to universities, do usual business, greet their neighbors, smile, shake hands, eat and do everything as normal human beings. The next moment, they are seen killing citizens with the rage of their guns and explosives, killing even themselves.* (*Flame* 24)

The book propagates also the message of peace and non-violence in a potent manner:

> *The eternal flame knows no occupation, faith nor complexion and cannot be imprisoned within human bonds. It has engulfed millions, whose names can be traced in every age and land. This flame is known to engulf mortals even today, melting unknown metals into one.* (*Flame* 28)

To Gill, hope is a sprinkler of peace in the dark cloudy nights and a potent vocalization of the eternal human value of peace. Again, 'it is the binding force for families, plants/

every atom/ and every part of every individual'. *The Flame* is the light of hope in the darkness of dejection. It provides solace in private agonies and binds people together with the cord of unity. Hope has been creeping in a calm manner throughout the poem and energizes constantly the poet even when he feels entirely shattered while portraying the picture of modern terrorism. Despite all the dismal and ugly pictures of the present-day world hag-ridden with terrorism and violence, *The Flame* has countless references where one can find Gill full of optimism, hope and vision for a better tomorrow.

Comments of Helen Bar-Lev, a prominent poet and artist from Israel, are to the point:

> *The Flame is a poem of tenderness, incomprehension, longing, anger, hope, and sadness. It is a poem which gives all the reasons for peace, and also the reasons we do not have it. Were there more Stephen Gills in this world. (Bar-Lev* 5)

The poet seems brimming with optimism when he forbids to 'Let the arrows of despair' hurt him and challenges 'if /The clouds, the hills/And the waterfalls/mock his attempts,' he will react in a different manner:

I shall catch
glimpses of your elegance
in the glow of the candles
within the temple that I build
for you. (Flame 132)

Poet's hope can be discerned in the following lines:

Sea waves
sing my song
and the rainbow colours
my amorous tale.
If I ever feel unfulfilled
I shall shed a few drops
to water the seedlings of my passion. (Flame 133)

Dove, a symbol of peace and non-violence, also seems mixed with hopefulness and radiance which is clearly visible in many of his trilliums (in Haiku Spirit) of his collection named *Flashes*. Dove actually propagates the message of hope:

Dove flies towards skies
green branch in beak
message of our hopes. (*Flashes* 33)

It (Dove) 'flies/ human sleep/ in the fold of dreams' and 'muses on a branch' with 'eyes half shut' and reaches beyond the boundaries:

Dove draws no boundaries
no fuss
gypsy of hopes. (*Flashes* 34)

In another collection *Songs Before Shrine*, Gill feels dove's melody echoing in his soul and instilling hope and vigour in him. He hears the dove's melody surging in his soul and watches its face and feels its beat in his flesh and blood. He writes:

I envision it flying
across my horizon;
I smell its presence
in the air. (13)

In another poem of the same collection, 'The Dove of Peace', it is nothing but hope that is making Stephen Gill say:

For a long time
I have been hearing
the dove of peace will be freed
shortly. (9)

He creates a mild but pricking irony:

To awaken that dove
progress has been made
today's comfort
more sacrificed
our homes now better adorned
with the thorns of hatred
a few more nuclear bombs
remain to be developed
and contested. (SBS 9)

In 'Man of Today', he sketches the shattered hope of peace and holds the man responsible for all the traumas. He seems grim to see 'songs of peace' on one hand and distribution of weapons / siding with the murderers on the other'. He asks:

On one side
respect for the cats
fondness for the dogs.
On the other side
defeat for humanity. (SBS 27).

In such adverse atmosphere of agony, injustice, and disharmony, the bud of hope is shrunk:

The wings of their dove
cracked and clipped
footprint of harmony erased
and hope-bud shrunk. (SBS 23)

Similarly in poem 'Evening of Harmony', the poet finds the 'sun of harmony sinking / in the cave of despair / as does the heart/ of a homeless orphan', and adds: *Inside the home / the fireplace of hopes burns / outside lurks a vacuum. (SBS* 16)

Despite all such deep disappointments, the poet never leaves hope, and his dove does not stop breathing in any adverse climate. He urges hopefully:

Let the gleams of your glory
ravage the plague of intolerance
for a new creature to emerge. (SBS 7)

The poet's dove 'strives / to play with her wings / while the brutal blades of nightmares / clip them. The poet is not woe-begone. He writes:

The dove's sight
is the melody of blessing
for the comfort of homes.
The dove's presence
is the rhythm of the creator. (*Shrine* 56)

He continues:

As the oracle of hope
the soul-soothing dove
sings
from her creative solitude. (Ibid.)

In 'My Dove', he finds the dove of longing sanctified in the sanctum of serenity' and is above all nations. He sees dove as perfect vehicle of peace and hope on the earth:

She radiates
hues of nondepictable truth
that consecrates
the emptiness of her surroundings.
The leaf that she carries
is from the evergreen tree
of never ending hope. (Shrine 149)

Keeping these fears, dejection and terrible atmosphere in mind, he prays for better days to come. He appeals:

Strengthen my voice to weed out
the fear

the sickness
and the satanic wrath of the past
and to help
truth to appear. (SBS 5)

The poet in Gill visions for better years in future. He asks the Almighty to 'pacify the frenzy of the violence' as well as equip poet's pen with 'amazement fused with vitality'. He wishes 'to harvest / a ripe manna of harmony / of the youthful enlightenment' and 'blossom a richness of pleasing nutrients/of calm energy'. His songs also come together with the hopeful movement of dove, he says:

Fragrance of spring
sustain a structure of strength
with the braces of my lyrics
that will secure breaths together
in a mystical dance
to the tune of the song of the dove. (SBS 2)

Mother is another icon of hope and sacrifice to Stephen Gill. Her loving care and memories always remain with the poet. He finds his mother in 'all three novels *Why, Immigrant* and *The Loyalist City* and dedicates his collection *Songs Before Shrine* to her. In his poem 'To Mother' he presents her as the perfect image of hope. He writes:

Image of sacrifice
message of hope
you are highly prized
the gift of the life
I owe to you. (SBS 1)

Gill is well aware of the hardships of life and knows the intensity of pain, loneliness and defeats. He writes:

Whole life I shaped my path
gusts of loneliness never stopped
light missing. (*Flashes* 52)

Yet he keeps on living without grumbling or murmuring:

No haste
no worry
no malice
and no darkness of prejudice
lurks here.
Eyes set on my horizon
on calm waves I sail here. (SBS 38)

Hoping for the arrival of the spring, he writes:

Youth will run and roam
flowers grow and bloom
trees will be graced
birds sing
and greenery abound. (SBS 83)

It is a time when 'songs arise/ hopes throb/ and madness spreads.' (SBS 83) The abundance of optimism, hope, peace, love and harmony make the poet hopeful for a glorious dawn in this age of adversaries. Dr. George Hines is right when he says: *The poet envisages a future in which all living things will cooperate in harmony and will 'smile together in life's field. (SGHW* 92).

Gill is aware of the duties and responsibilities of a true poet. Poets are the sentinel of the conscience who draw a vivid and transparent picture of the society and point out the foibles of human character. Gill knows when a poet is needed:

When dearth and sword
and hope despaired
sound their notes
•poet is acclaimed
and sought. (SBS 39)

Gill knows that the 'poets are adventurous' who 'dive

with swimmers / dance with singers / and enter / the souls of tyrant/ as they paint/ voyaging / in the seas of thoughts flowing/ the waters of emotions / with the delicate oars / of pens'. For him poets are the givers of happiness. They should not die in the dark and despair. His plea is right:

Should poets
let the flower of hope be wasted
by the sickles of racial winds
is the question now? (SBS 29)

In 'Birth of Poems', from his collection *Songs Before Shrine,* he expects much hope from poets:

Poets free
the birds of their blood
and
weave purrs and growls. (32)

Stephen Gill has high hopes with poetry. He considers his own poems as 'the brooks / that flow leisurely / through the green valleys / of blessedness'. He considers that his poetry can 'root out terrorists/ that sail on the currents of cruelty'. His poetry is a constant struggle for peace and for human rights.

His poetry finds the 'rhythm of life/ within the castle of grace' and 'cannot be abducted'. According to him, his poetry is the mine of hopes.

My songs
beauty in living
hope for warmth
and thirst of prosperity.
The rainbow of my joy
link distant islands of disharmony. (SBS 43)

Stephen Gill shows his deep craving for hope and optimism which can be glanced in the following lines:

If there were dreams for sale
I would be the first to buy
no matter how high the price. (SBS 69)

He further says: *I'll pay any price/ for the dreams that lighten the burden/ brighten the day with sunrise... (*SBS 69*).* In many of his poems, Stephen Gill states that our present sorrows are temporary. Man should try to develop his environment with love, peace, truth and higher human values and renovate his soul with the beaming light of fresh hope. He emphasizes that to establish spirituality man should also follow the natural laws. Concerning poetry of Gill it is justified to quote George Hines's words:

> *Just as the sun melts the morning mist, the poet hopes for a spiritual sun which will melt the ignorance, fear, hatred and greed which are 'deeply amassed around our necks. (SGHW* 92)

Stephen Gill's poetry is a combination of hopes and despairs. In crystal clear images of contemporary life of destructive complexities and cut-throat competitions that lead the citizens of today to mental disturbance, psychological imbalance and spiritual 'insolence, Gill lits the lamps of hope. These lamps will definitely illuminate the paths of future generations. Though his poems are full of dismal pictures of terrorism and its consequences, yet they encourage man to ride through the rough tempestuous sea and cross all the boundaries of callous calamities and dreadful disasters. Stephen Gill knows well that written words create miracles but for that sacrifice is needed.

In his interview with N.K. Agarwal he says:

> *I write to disseminate my message in an art form. This is a process of burning oneself or going through the pains of a pregnant mother. (Kafla* 49)

The poetic goblet of Gill is filled with hope to the brim in his poems. He says: *I hope my writings about peace will cause change in the thinking of my readers.* (*Kafla* 49) Such writings, full of optimism and certitude, will confer inner peace to the individual and an alternative succor to his agonized soul by inspiring him to bind each and every human being in the sacred bonds of love, fraternity, peace and global brotherhood. This is a way for human progeny to lead a better life.

Works Cited

Bar-Lev, Helen. "Stephen_Gill's Poem *The Flame* gives all the reasons for peace", www.stephengill.ca/gazette.htm

Dickinson, Emily. *The Complete Poems of Emily Dickinson.* Johnson, Thomas H. (ed.) Cambridge: Harvard University Press, 1955.

Gill, Stephen, *Shrine,* Allahabad: Cyberwit.net, 2008.

–. *Songs Before Shrine.* New Delhi: Authorspress, 2007. (Abbreviated as *SBS* in the text.)

–. *Flashes.* New Delhi: Imprint, 2007.

–. *The Flame.* Canada: Vesta Publications, 2008.

Hines, George, *Stephen Gill and His Works,* New Delhi: Authors Press,2008 (Abbreviated as *SGHW* in the text.)

Kafla Inter-Continental, No. 36, IICA, Dev Bhardwaj, (ed.) Chandigarh. Jan-April 2008, 'Stephen Gill on his Writings and Diaspora' an interview by N.K. Agarwal.

8

The Maniac Messiahs in Stephen Gill's *The Flame*

G. Dominic Savio and S.J. Kala

> *"A shoot will come up from the stump of Jesse; from his roots a Branch will bear fruit..."*
>
> – *Isaiah* 11:1-10

> *"And he will be called Wonderful Counselor, Mighty God, Everlasting Father, Prince of Peace*
>
> – *Isaiah* 9:1-7

> *"And Ma'amin, I believe with a full heart in the coming of the Messiah, and even though he may tarry, I will wait for him on any day that he may come."*
>
> *Maimonides's Thirteen Principles of Faith*

'Messiah', is a Hebrew word, meaning the 'anointed one'. It is an oft used term in Judaism and in Christianity. The followers of both the religions have a deep faith in Messiah. But, they differ from one another in their beliefs. According to the Jews, the Messiah's reign lies in the future. They eagerly await it unlike the Christians who believe Jesus Christ to be their Messiah.

The messiahs of Judaism and Christianity have always featured in many literary works. They have either a close or a remote semblance to either of them. But, presently a messiah with a vast difference and a rare one, a maniac is depicted by Stephen Gill in his long poem, *The Flame.* The phrase "maniac messiahs" used by this multiple-award-winning poet appears to have a purpose. Probably it throws out the lava of disgust from the volcano of suppressed wrath kindled at the unquestionable happenings in this abominable hell, the world.

Stephen Gill, a Punjabi Christian presently in Canada, has witnessed great socio-political turmoil during the Indo-Pakistan Partition. The continual clash between the Hindus and the Muslims that led to social disturbances and the killing of innumerable innocents has left an indelible imprint on his mind. The imprint is etched out with due pain in almost all his literary creations, viz., novels, poems and critical essays.

The suffering undergone then prods him to patronize Peace and Universal Brotherhood in all his writings. World Federalism, a concept that he promotes and craves for is propagated through his works. *The Flame* (2008), a collection of cantos, showcasing Stephen Gill's social concerns and yearning for peace, brings out the harrowing experiences of the victims of the diabolic terrorism. The subtitle, "A long poem about the destruction caused by maniac messiahs", makes the reader contemplate on who the messiahs are and why they are labelled so.

This paper focuses the maniac messiahs in *The Flame.* It aims at juxtaposing the maniac messiahs in *The Flame* with the Christian and Judaic messiahs and studies their contradictions. It also delves deeper into the nomenclature, the prophecies in *the Bible* and the characteristics of the Christian messiah.

In the article on "The Messiah" from Jewish virtual library, it is understood that the belief in messiah and a messianic age is so deeply rooted in Jewish tradition. (1) The Jews in Babylonia who were on an exile during the sixth century BC hoped for a messiah an "anointed one" to bring them home. Soon, they found the messiah in the Persian King Cyrus Great who facilitated their return home in 539. In the second century BCE they suffered from repression and they looked forward for a messiah especially in the form of a military leader who would free them from all subjugations and defeat their Roman enemies.

They also believed that he would establish an independent Jewish kingdom. Gradually there was a change in their belief system. The Jews were made to believe that their messiah may not be a military leader but may be a charismatic teacher who would interpret the Mosaic Law correctly, restore Israel and judge mankind. Within a century they discovered such a charismatic teacher in Jesus of Nazareth.

But, the Jews refused to accept him as the messiah. The reasons for the non–acceptance of Jesus of Nazareth as their messiah is that "he did not usher in world peace, as Isaiah had prophesied.... In addition Jesus did not help bring about Jewish political sovereignty for the Jews or protection from their enemies." (*The Messiah* 2)

After Jesus Christ, many Palestinian Jews revolted against the Romans under the headship of their messiah, Simon Barkokhba. Its effects were dreadful. Quite contrary to the belief of the traditional Jews in a personal messiah, Reform Judaism, a movement of the modern world denies the arrival of an individual messiah. It insists on "a future world in which human efforts, not a divinely sent messenger, will bring about a utopian age." (*The Messiah* 2)

"The Hebrew word *masiah* means 'anointed one' and may indicate Jewish priests, prophets and kings" (Lendering 1). In Greek, messiah was translated as *Christos* hence the Christian Messiah was called "Jesus the Christ". Neither traits of Jewish priests, prophets and kings nor that of Christ can be seen in "the maniac messiahs" of Stephen Gill in his *The Flame.*

The Flame, a long poem is written in eight parts and sixty two cantos which describes the devastation caused by the maniac messiahs. The first part of the poem is devotional. It is in the second, third, fourth and the fifth that he highlights the destruction wrought by the terrorists. In the sixth part Gill sketches out the silhouettes of those who are responsible of the calamity. The seventh and the eighth part of the poem are earnest craving for the loss, both physical and psychological.

In the blurb, Gill declares that *The Flame* is not an attack on any particular community, religion or nationality. He opines that "people are people everywhere and suffering is suffering". The bombing of a Day Care Centre in *The Flame* is a well schemed act of the terrorists. The crazy, foolish and insane acts that are unjustifiable on any grounds even in a fantasied world earn him the title of "the maniac messiahs", conferred by Gill. Why then should they be called so? A look at the roots of the concept and the belief in it might be of immense help to the study. Furthermore, are Gill's "the maniac messiahs" an upshot of any other recent movement? How close or distant are they to / from the Christian and Judaic messiahs?

A study of the messianic expectations of the Christians and orthodox and non-orthodox Jews is quintessential. Only then can "the maniac messiahs" in Stephen Gill's *The Flame* be understood well. According to Judaism, Maimonides summarises what the Messiah is expected to do as follows:

> *... He will be a descendent of David*
> *He does not have to perform signs or wonders...*
> *He will fight the wars of the Lord*
> *Elijah will come before Messiah....*
> *In messiah's reign there will be no hunger or wars...*
> (The Messiah of Judaism 3)

In the *Old Testament* there are umpteen messianic prophecies. Christians believe that the advent of Christ is foretold in the *Old Testament* and it is realized in the *New Testament*. According to the key reference in the *Old Testament* historical books, the prophecies in "Psalms" which consist of praise songs, the *book of Job* and that of the major and Minor Prophets, the characteristics of the Messiah is as follows:

...He'll battle with Satan
He'll have both priestly and kingly roles
The messiah will be a redeemer, and will live on earth
The messiah is God's son; the messiah is divine
The messiah will suffer at the hands of his detractors...
The messiah will usher in a new era of peace and tranquility...
He will bear the sins of many
He will perform miracles... (Jones 14)

Having analysed the characteristics of Judaic Messiahs and the Christian Messiah, an intrinsic investigation of the characteristics of the maniac messiahs in *The Flame* is to be carried out.

Gill in his preface to *The Flame* introduces the term "the maniac messiahs". He identifies them as those "misled individuals who generate the blizzards of fear and panic." (*The Flame* 7) He does not come out with evident explanations of why he calls them so. The readers wonder whether it is because of the self attribution of the characteristics of the messiahs of the Christian and orthodox and non - orthodox Jews by the terrorists. The manic messiahs "call themselves liberators, separatists and jehadis" (*The Flame* 20).

Who are these maniac messiahs? According to Gill they are the openers of Pandora's Box. True to the scientific world, they make immense use of Science and Technology to create the intended chaos. They are "educated and illiterate, rich and poor, men and women, politicians, engineers, medicos and religious leaders of all ages" (*The Flame* 25). Where do these maniac messiahs come from? Like Jesus have they come out of Judah? Or like the Messiah of Judaism, are they a descendent of David? No, they are not so. Gill clearly states that they are from every community and background (*The Flame* 20-21). The terrorists have no distinguished roots of their own. In reality as well as in *The Flame* there is no special reference to their background.

It is believed that the Messiah will fight against Satan or will wage the wars of the Lord. Nevertheless, the maniac messiahs fight a battle that is altogether different from the battle of the Christian and the Judaic messiahs. They battle directly with law abiding citizens, the civilians. Thereby, they pressurise their government to accept their agenda, an indirect battle.

Their relentless pursuit
to grab the crown of chaos
swim political pendulums ....(The Flame 103)

The terrorists wage this war with the lethal weapons of violence and the threat of violence.

... their deal
with the devil
the sightless assassins of the innocents ... (The Flame 90)

Wanton violence
startled signals to stamp out
the plague
that scourges the defenseless lives. (The Flame 100)

The deal of the maniac messiahs with the devil is divergent to the belief of the Christians and the Jews in the messiah battling with the Satan. The deal with the devil also has allusions to Faustus' deal with Mephistopheles.

The Christian prophesies foretell of the messiah having to perform both priestly and kingly roles. What roles do the maniac messiahs in *The Flame* have to play? According to Gill the maniac messiahs have variegated roles to perform. Firstly, they play the role of destroyers. They actively engage themselves in destroying many. Accordingly they are the bringer of deaths and casualties to the innocent civilians.

... the avatars of savagery
mow down defenseless innocents (The Flame 48)

Time stopped when an explosion
blew up... (51)

Many lost their eyes,
ears and fingers
bones broken and twisted
rambled in shock
among the debris and dead bodies. (The Flame 52)

After engaging themselves in destruction they hardly realize the ineffaceable physical and psychological impacts it can cause.

several families did not speak
and several more confused, outraged or shocked
sat frozen (The Flame 84)

Shocked volunteers
witnessed a pyramid of ashes
over the cradles –
a bone-chilling calculation (The Flame 78)

Secondly, the maniac messiahs play the role of a trainer or a brainwasher with the responsibility of conducting "secret training camps", where they exercise for physical fitness, learn to use firearms, explosives and receive constant doses for their brainwash.

For which evidence
of what study
they rambled through the last hours ...(The Flame 94)

in the windowless cells
of anarchistic gospel
they prepare terror
with the weeds of ignorance
on the fire of savagery...(The Flame 104)

The above-quoted lines reveal conspicuously the scheming that has preceded the noxious act. It is apparent that the plotting takes place "in the windowless cells". Thirdly they are the industrialists running the industry of terrorism. The monthly or the annual mammoth turnover of the industry is the fund utilized for all their activities. They generate a treasure trove from the "sale of drugs, and the misuse of the funds of some charitable organizations formed to deceive people and governments" (21). Gill underscores it in his poem *The Flame:*

In the plutonium trade
smuggles are more likely
by these dukes of fruitless longing. (The Flame 104)

With knowledge,
easy money and weight
they become maniac messiahs
to snuff out the inner blaze. (The Flame 102)

Lastly and most significantly they are diabolic warriors who fight with innocent civilians using the poisonous weapons of violence and the threat of it.

... to widen the ditches of agonies
and spread a carpet of paralyzing fear
to mangle mothers
and wives. (The Flame 102)

The phrase "Spread a carpet of paralyzing fear" underlines Gill's views of the terrorists attempts in spreading the threat of violence. Is this threat by the maniac messiahs a forewarning of the forthcoming peril? It is indeed worth pondering. However, the rigorous training that these terrorists receive to indulge in violence and to be in the vanguard of the battle turns them into heartless souls. Nothing can make them little warm.

I ask blood spillers
from the cabaret of appalling barbarity
if they hear

the silence of infants
in the cradles of terror;
share
the woes of mothers (The Flame 89)

The maniac messiahs play different roles with perfection. What is their driving force? Why do they aim at "soft targets", the civilians? "They do this work for a greater good or for themselves to enter the kingdom of their land of peace easily" (*The Flame* 25). It is undoubtedly outrageous that they too talk of peace. Gill's deliberations on the different theories of peace expose the readers to an unashamed truth that "Terrorists also talk of peace. They believe that they achieve or will achieve peace by terrorizing citizens" (*The Flame* 20). But, ironical enough, they do not bring the assured peace to anyone. "Those who believe in preparation for war for peace have invented the deadliest weapons such as nuclear bombs. Instead of peace, the world is coming closer to the threshold of complete annihilation" (*The Flame* 20).

They usher in only chaos and commotion. They fail to be redeemers.

... and in the lonely corridor of the evening
discomforting silence wander
wearing
a despairing mantle of confusion. (The Flame 79)

Unlike the religious messiahs, the manic messiahs lack priestly authority. They are mostly prodded by religious fanaticism and they are neither truly religious nor spiritual. Obviously they are hardly humane in their attempts to reach their goals. They are solely guided by their limitless craze for power that they would wield in making others subservient to them.

It is alleged that the messiah is divine and is God's son. But, maniac messiahs cannot be imagined to be God's son nor can divinity be ever associated with these earthly maniac messiahs of Gill in *The Flame*. A divine spirit can hardly imagine of such destruction:

Car bombs, mobility and might
have become the toys of the robots
who know how and when
to free their unfed tigers
from the cages of depravity. (*The Flame* 102)

Only an uncivilized and a cold-blooded human being can be the cause of such an explosion mentioned in *The Flame.* When they are the cause of many sufferings, how then can they be suffering messiahs? One of the messianic expectations is that the messiah will be a sufferer at the hands of his detractors. Here, in *The Flame,* the maniac messiahs are not the sufferers instead they are the source of meaningless sufferings and unbearable pain:

... babies
shrouded in blood
and plastered with insulation
or faces half covered with glass
calling brokenly
for their dads and moms (*The Flame* 72)

What harm did the innocent babies cause the maniac messiahs? Why is it that they become the target? Are they not affected in any way? All these inexplicable questions arise when one mulls over the inexcusable disaster:

The place
where the dismembered limbs lie
mocks the blindness of the brutes (*The Flame* 97)

The line "mocks the blindness of the brutes" is self-explanatory. It reveals about the self-centered and barbaric temperament of the terrorists.

Another vital characteristic of a Messiah is that he will be rejected by some of his own people. With this parameter the maniac messiahs are gauged. Who are close t the maniac messiahs? Only their followers! The rest of the people dread them because of the threat of violence and the violence caused by them. They detest them for their mean nature of disregarding human life. In *The Flame* the pains undergone by people of different age groups have been well documented:

Indignant waves
of sadness and fury
of every group and race....(The Flame 96)

...children
... suffer from the painful longing
... parents have gone
to soothe their sagging spirit
The morning

... that buried your elders
in a massive grave of frozen mind... (The Flame 97)

Will anyone be closer to the maniac messiahs after such a catastrophe? Certainly they will like to be far from them by rejecting them. It is to be noticed that the maniac messiahs are not rejected by some people only but all other than their cohorts. A Christian Messiah is expected to perform miracles.

According to *Oxford Dictionary*, a miracle is an "act or event (some thing good or welcome) which does not follow the known laws of nature; remarkable and surprising event". Instead in Gill's *The Flame*, the maniac messiahs blow away the Day Care Centre. It is not a good or a welcome act. It is an act against the laws of the society. The devastation catches people unaware. Contrasting the maniac messiahs with the religious messiahs it is understood that they are hate incarnate. The guiding star of all their activities is hate and only hate. Their disgusting behaviour exhibits their anger towards and odium for their government and the civilians.

The heavenly bodies
must have wept in disgrace

for their impotent rage to burst
the blisters of shocking atrocities
wrapped in a shroud of secrecy. (*The Flame* 90)

... to appease Beelzebub
with their offerings
at the altar of a seething cauldron of wrath (*The Flame* 91)

... who had tried to frame a coffin
for liberty
under the shades of their vilest
impulses. (*The Flame* 97)

The phrases "seething cauldron of wrath" and "vilest impulses" talks of the abominable nature of the terrorists. Their hatred and anger is manifested in the explosion, "the blisters of shocking atrocities" that was planned in "secrecy".

A Messiah is said to bear the sins of many. Ludicrously, there needs to be someone who will bear the sins of the maniac messiahs. Who is it going to be? The countless number of crimes that they commit saddles them with their own grave sins. In such a condition how will they bear others' sins? In an attempt to bear the sins of many a Messiah will be persecuted. However, preposterously the maniac messiahs persecute others.

... hands, legs
and blood all around. ...
they collected them
in separate bags. ...

An attendant tagged
the feet of twenty infants
on the first day. (*The Flame* 76)

The "... hands, legs and blood" and "the feet of twenty infants" vouch for the mayhem caused by the maniac messiahs. It is sure that such maniac messiahs will not bring salvation to any. Nor will they ever usher in a new era of peace and tranquillity.

Yet another distinguishing trait of a Messiah is that he will be the final judge. The maniac messiahs in *The Flame* are to some extent judges. They seem to judge the fate of others by taking away the God given life from them. They decide on the end of others. Is it because of this that Stephen Gill labels them maniac messiahs? Is it because of the only rationale that they foresee the death of others that they are called so? Does the word "maniac" in the phrase "maniac messiahs" have any underlying current? A quick look at the word the "maniac" will facilitate a better understanding of the phrase and the character of the terrorists. The Oxford Dictionary explains it as an "extreme enthusiast". Wikipedia the free encyclopedia identifies him to be "A person who exhibits the behaviour known as mania" and also says that he can be classified as a serial killer. Mania is a type of ruthless medical condition that is characterized by exceptionally elevated mood, energy, unusual thought patterns. The dictionary meaning can better be taken up for studying the phrase "maniac messiahs" instead of the medical explanation as such a patient will certainly need a clinical treatment. The "maniac messiahs" in Stephen Gill's *The Flame* are "extreme enthusiasts". They are nothing more than a sort of serial killer. They indulge in mass killing.

> *... before unchaining the bulldozers*
> *of their delusional disorder*
> *to create a tormenting lake...* (*The Flame* 90)
>
> *... preparing a lurid feast*
> *to feed their famished fascination....*
>
> *They tied the knots of reason*
> *before plunging bayonets*
> *into the raw flesh...* (*The Flame* 91)

The phrases "famished fascination" and "delusional

disorder" showcase the maniac messiahs as "extreme enthusiasts" and throw light on their insanity.

> *... soft opiates to their mind*
> *they grabbed and gazed*
> *baffling over the potentials*
> *of savagery it wombed (The Flame* 92)

A reading of the above lines explains why Stephen Gill has used the word maniac. For these maniacs, "extreme enthusiasts" destruction is the only motto. Logic is a rare tool that they make use of. From the line "... soft opiates to their mind" the readers understand how blind they are to reasoning.

Why did Gill ever use the word messiah? Is it because the terrorists feel that they are working for a mission with a vision? Is it because they too talk of peace and a promised land of peace? Is it because they decide the fate of many innocent victims? Whatever be the reason they can in no way be compared with any religious messiahs and Gill is also very clear about it. Gill seems to be comforting himself by addressing them with the sugar – coated phrase the "maniac messiah". He has wisely used the adjective "maniac" with the noun "messiah". Gill, being an advocate of peace, deals with the terrorists too in a mild fashion. Instead of going in for tooth for tooth and an eye for eye, he showcases his true Christian spirit in addressing the dealers of vice as "maniac messiahs". Had Gill been very unsympathetic in his dealing, he would have ceased to be a Christian. Even the terrorists themselves will be moved for a while and may have second thought about their evil doings when they come to know that they are addressed as "maniac messiahs". If this phrase can create such a wonder then Gill's dreams of promoting peace through literature and building a universe of peace cannot be far away.

References

Gill, Stephen, *The Flame,* Canada: Vesta Publications, 2008.

Jones, Robert, "The Messiah - In the Old Testament, the Apocrypha, and the Dead Sea Scrolls" 17 Aug. 2008 <www.sundayschoolcourses.com/messiah/index.htm>

Lendering, Jona, "Messiah (overview)" 17 Aug. 2008 <www.livius.org/men-mh/messiah/messiah00.html>

"Messiah (Handel)" WikipediaThe Free Encyclopedia. 17 Aug. 2008 <en.wikipedia.org/wiki/Messiah_(Handel)>

"Messiah" WikipediaThe Free Encyclopedia. 17 Aug. 2008 <en.wikipedia.org/wiki/Messiah>

"The Messiah of Judaism" 17 Aug. 2008 <www.truthnet.org/TheMessiah/4_Messiah_of_Judaism/>

"The Messiah" Jewish Virtual Library_17 Aug. 2008 <www.jewishvirtuallibrary.org/jsource/Judaism/messiah.html>

9

Stephen Gill's *The Flame:* Poetry for a Cause

Ashok Kumar

John Milton (1608-74) was a great poet. Greatness is writ large in his writings. His life, works, religious and political beliefs placed him higher than others. But, when he composed the sonnet 'When the Assault was intended' in 1642, he was verbally assaulted by the critics. It was a poetic appeal for mercy. The Royalists forces were marching towards the city of London after their victory of Edge hill over the Puritan troops in the civil war. Milton, who was a Puritan and a supporter of Parliamentary democracy, feared an attack on his house at the Alders gate Street by Royalists forces. Hence, he appealed:

Lift not thy spear against the Muses' bower
The great Emathian conqueror bid spare
The house of Pindarus, when temple and tower
Went to the ground: and the repeated air
Of sad Electra's poet had the power
To save the Athenians walls from ruin bare.

(*The Golden Treasury* 75-76)

To Milton, poetry of highest order meant sublime theme and lofty ideals. Poetry must not be used as a means to dispel fear or to beg mercy for life. Stephen Gill's *The Flame* (2008) sends a message to all to shun violence. The basic question once again recurs how far is it justified to compose a poem or any literary work for a personal or a social cause? Does it not belittle the poet and the poem? Literature must not be a vehicle for propaganda. There are hundreds of peace-missions, saints and philosophers who are busy in spreading the message of peace and non-violence. I humbly register a strong protest against the poetry of propaganda.

Let us examine Stephen Gill's poetic work *The Flame* which is a long narrative in verse and has sixty two cantos spread in eight parts. First few parts are devotional in which Gill like transcendentalists finds divinity in all objects of this universe.

You are
the beat that echoes
in the breast of the arc
you meditate
in the melody of the falls. (The Flame 33)

At another place in Part I, the poet feels the soothing effect of the divine presence in the objects of nature:

You are the quietness
over the meadows
where
the lush vegetation sprawl
in the gulf of the spring.
The keenness of insight
beats within the hyacinths
of your smiles. (The Flame 43)

In the second part of *The Flame* he condemns those who have become the avatars of savagery:

When
the avatars of savagery
mow down defenseless innocents
and
tear down the towers of routine
deep pain goes deeper
inside. (*The Flame* 48)

During the last fifty years world has suffered much violence and has seen a lot of bloodshed perpetrated by religious bigots, terrorists and separatists. Perhaps, some people think that they can subdue the world by violence. Gill has tried to show how the bombs have been exploded and destruction has been done by "maniac messiahs" at the places of worship. Here is a specimen of his observation:

Time stopped when an explosion
blew up the simple elegance
of my flame.
The furious rumbling bang
released a sudden cataclysm
that the devotees thought.
an earthquake. (*The Flame* 51)

He also shows the damage:

Many lost their eyes
ears and fingers
bones broken and trusted
rambled in shock
among the debris and dead bodies. (*The Flame* 52)

Gill also shows the effect of violence on human psyche in Part IV.

After weeks in the hospital
the infant returned home
with a tube to breathe.

For his grandmother
it was awakening
from a bad dream. (*The Flame* 71)

In Part V of the book, Gill gives a picture of the rescue efforts. Mark Gill's keen observation:

A camp was extemporized
in a marking lot
to anatomize
the shattered shell
floor by floor
indicating the bodies
that could not be pulled out . . .
Soaked in blood
nurses in uniform
rushed around the improvised surgeries
. . .
The area was cordoned off
most exit ramps were closed
the telephone lines jammed
the car agencies
had nothing to sent
investigators and relatives
filled the hotels. (*The Flame* 81)

The poet asks the maniac messiahs to listen to the voice of children, mothers and wives after perpetrating violence in the name of religions, race or sect. Perhaps they may realize what they have done. Stephen Gill asks in Part VI:

I ask blood spiller
from the cabaret of appalling barbarity
if they hear
the silence of infants
in the cradles of terror; (*The Flame* 89)

The poet gives a vivid description of destruction in which

young and old have lost their lives or rendered cripple by the blast made by bomb or RDX. He uses a documentary device to present different aspects of terrorists strike at a place. A train of events beginning from police and ambulance and ending with T.V., Radio and press journalists has been presented with keen insight. He observes that today's world is living under the cloud of fear and insecurity. He fails to see beauty of Almighty's creation because:

I can not see
the burning bush of your beauty
because terrorists have loosened
suffocating gases
from the sea of their insanity. (The Flame 106)

But the poet in Gill is optimistic as he believes that the world would overcome this state of fear and suffering by the bliss of God:

We need the grace of your presence
to weed out the bigotry
the cruelty
the fanatic howls
the fear
the sickness
and for mosaic to refine its gem
for equality to shine. (The Flame 110)

The poet's flame is not fire. It is light of knowledge, light of truth and so on. It is rather divine. Gill elaborates it in Part VIII

Flame
is the binding force
for families, planets
every atom
and every part of every individual.
Life disintegrates

where the rays of flame
do not reach. (*The Flame* 135)

Sudhir K. Arora in 'Stephen Gill's Indian imagination: *The Flame*' finds *Gyan Yoga* and *Bhakti Yoga* as the cure for the melody of violence and terrorism. The *Gyan Marg* creates an illusion which makes a man see power through materialism while the *Bhakti Marg* removes illusion of materialism and reveals the true power that lies in peace which is the result of spiritualism.

When we take the total corpus of Stephen Gill into consideration, we find that Gill has undertaken the task of spreading peace as his mission of life. Everyone, who has studied Stephen Gill, has also discovered his struggle in an alien country. A feeling of alienation and insecurity has always been a part of his existence. A creative artist needs an atmosphere of peace and calm mind. Prof. A.N. Dwivedi comments:

> *"Stephen Gill, as a sensitive poet, is fully aware of these disturbing problems leading to insurmountable tension and crises in human minds. He suggests with a streak of idealism that peace and harmony are the thinkable remedies for them" (11).*

To sum up, Stephen Gill's *The Flame* is a significant work and definitely an improvement over his previous works. He has very carefully employed non-traditional analogies and metaphors which give *The Flame* a new look. It is a good example of labored poetry. Stephen Gill himself believed that poetry is 90 per cent perspiration and 10 per cent inspiration. He does not believe that poetry is born out of divine impulse. He says: "There is a myth that poetry strikes a poet like a flash or it is a divine bolt" (*The Flame* 17). He believes in working and working on a poem again and again till it gets a perfect shape and a form.

In English literature, Matthew Arnold is the best example of labored poetry. Though he did not enjoy the talents of Wordsworth, Shelly and Keats, he tried to reach the pinnacles of poetry. At heart, Arnold was a romantic and at the theoretical level he was a classicist. These are my views and I do not impose on anyone, however, literature is replete with poets whose poetry can be called laboured poetry. Some of them have achieved success. Stephen Gill may be yet another name added to this category.

References

Arora, Sudhir K., "Stephen Gill's Indian imagination in the Flame," *The Indian Journal of English Studies,* XLVI, 2009: 219.

Dwivedi, A.N., "Fissures and Factures: Identity Crisis in Gill's Poetry," *Discovering Stephen Gill,* ed. N.K. Agarwal, New Delhi: Authorspress, 2008.

Gill, Stephen. *The Flame.* Canada: Vesta Publication, 2008.

Milton, John, "When the Assault Was Intended to the City," *The Golden Treasury,* 75-76.

10

Invisible Issues in Stephen Gill's *Shrine*

Nidhish Kumar Singh

A Poet Laureate of Ansted University and Former Vice-President of World Federalists of Canada, Stephen Gill has authored more than twenty books, including collections of poems, fiction, literary criticism and the books of historical nature. He has not only written in English but also in Punjabi, Urdu and Hindi languages. His several poems have been translated in German, Spanish, Bengali, and other languages.

The experiences of the environment in which an author breathes cast a valuable effect on his/her writing as well. The 'personal experiences of a poet create his poetic voice' (Agarwal 93). Gill's writings show his bitter experiences of life full of worse circumstances, stuffing environment and the ailing humanity. His writings exhibit his voice of protest against these experiences. The partition fury rooted deep in the heart of Gill shakes his heart with every gust and it has tamed his conscience and often bothered him. His quest for remedy ends in the final refuge of Muse. She greets him with creative power to vent his fury and feeling. He turns the sparks into flames which illuminate the things that the darkness has devoured. The specialty of Gill as a poet is that he can see the things that are behind the light like stars behind the sun. The poet polishes them in a way that they eclipse the sun, so is Stephen Gill. He has shown the untouched things of Partition, war, revolts, terrorism, addiction, conflicts, etc. in his poetic collection *Shrine*. Chhote Lal Khatri remarks:

> *The volume consists of sixty poems on various aspects of social life – the problem of drug addiction, refugee, war, terrorism, atrocities on women and children, communalism and aids.* (Glimpses 188-189)

There are several Indians who have written on Partition of India and Pakistan, but Gill's approach is slightly different from them. He is also one of the victims of the Partition and has experienced it entirely. Therefore, his approach is more realistic as it originates from depth, sincerity and mildness. He kindles the horror of partition in his preface. He says:

> *Every time there was a stir caused by the wind, a car on the street, the bark of dog, or the mew of a cat, we froze inside our house. (Shrine* 8)

He adds further:

> *It was not easy to sleep when night after night the ghosts of fear looked straight into our eyes. (Shrine* 8)

Gill's preface to the *Shrine* is a documentary of Partition. He soundly elaborates the bewilderment, agony, torture, fear, frustration and the riot of parting India. He has fetched the things that are confined into the mind of a victim. His description successfully stirs the things that are still. The historical event is still alive in his nostalgic poems. It is the darkness that everyone wants to escape from but it still haunts Gill as his shadow. He admits:

> *It was a shock when I realized that the darkness I left behind had been chasing me continuously. The thought of cruelty of humans always remained in my mind like my own shadow. (Shrine* 23-24)

The impact of Partition brings Gill to the point where he gets an opportunity to know them. He thinks of war which is a curse to humanity. Gill demonstrates the invisible consequences of war through his poems. It cannot be the solution of any dispute – it illustrates only disaster, destruction, darkness, discomfort, bewilderment, crisis, insecurity, anger, jealousy etc. He writes in "War Fever" that war:

poisons the air of surroundings
disturbs the calm of sea
crumbles human relations
kills the appetite of the soul
weakens the liver of love
turning everything upside down. (*Shrine* 49)

Indeed, it cannot give solace to anyone. It becomes a cause of departing peace, harmony, justice, kindness, courtesy, charity and honey of humanity. Its hounds "ravage the bridge of harmony" and prohibit harmony and "dove of peace" to enter in our world. War leaves "poor shrunken things" in our mind and:

Bodies rotting in ditches
or dumped with the garbage.
Bodies washing up
onto the beaches
like bundles of clothes (*Shrine* 68)

It can be the matter of power, glory, pride, and prestige for politicians or nations, but it cannot be so for innocents. The innocent suffer most during and after war. They are deprived of their basic needs, including food, shelter, sanitation and medicine. They lose their son, brother, father, husband, daughter, mother, wife, sister and friends and become refugees, immigrants and victims of other miseries. Gill depicts the agony of a mother thus:

Here is a mother
who moves the corpses
to find her son; (Shrine 69)

He further adds:

Who are these innocents
whom the storm of cruelty
has extinguished
as of they were candles. (Shrine 69)

It is for this reason that he feels himself hostage even in his own house:

Alert in the bunker of panic
I like a hostage
to the ghastly Gulf War
that raises
the high walls of the captivity
to my freedom and peace
in my own living room
though I am thousands of miles
afar. (Shrine 53)

Terrorism is one of the major causes that disturb peace and social harmony. What Gill exhibits through his poetry, is entirely different. He offers the taste of the still waters of deep Ocean to those readers who are only acquainted with the taste of surface water.

Like literature it also has its latent and manifest aspects. We are acquainted with its manifest meaning but scarcely know about its latent content. Gill dips deep to find out the latent content and represents it through his poems. Terrorists are like the machines with parched hearts. Hence, they have become emotionless. Either they are dead for the world or the world is dead for them. Therefore, "they rape/ the sanctity of life" and slaughter men like carrot. The poet asks:

Why
they are trained
in the school of anarchy
which blooms
as deadly nightshade
on the fringes of fallacies.
Why
they talk of harmony
but plan genocide (Shrine 155)

Gill arouses some more significant questions that direct men to find the root of terrorism. He takes world as a nation, so to him, the problem of terrorism does not belong to a state, city, or region. Therefore, one should not cut its branches or trunk, but should endeavour to exterminate it from its roots. He insists that terrorists should be chained like mad dogs:

It is beyond
the shadow of my doubts
the law of the Jungle
and the language of weapons
are mad dogs
to be chained. (Shrine 156)

He also warns them:

Those who kiss
the lips of the sword
fall victims to its fury. (Shrine 156)

It is beyond the poet's perception why they choose arms and create violence for the settlement of disputes. Instead of solving, such a violent way enhances the problems. So, Gill does not advocate it:

I do not believe
in suppressing the truth

nor using arms
to settle disputes. (*Shrine* 157)

Gill focuses on the other side of the simplest but the serious causes of problem whether it is about war or terrorism or religion or addiction or politics or humanity. War and terrorism are the major demons that disturb world peace and harmony. Politicians play significant role in the settlement of the causes that breed the war-like circumstances. Gill brings into light the action they really take for the settlement:

Our rulers talk of peace
but it is futile
when nuclear-powered marines
sail over breasts of the oceans;
missiles look down like hawks
and neutrons
make fun of every life. (*Shrine* 46)

In the poems, 'The Voice of Democracy', 'Lotus of Freedom', and 'Seed of Democracy', Gill tells the politician that the lotus of freedom cannot bloom in stuffing environment. They have to be provided favourable environment for its growth. Gill says:

Cruelty can uproot a weed
but to uproot it – no!
Only autocrats will do it
to cause irreparable loss
to the stems of humanity. (*Shrine* 62)

If politicians want to sprout the lotus, they have to plant it where it should be:

I dwelt in those waters
where I received warmth
from the breeze of liberty.
The hands of the judiciary

caressed me,
singing a murmuring lullaby. (*Shrine* 59)

And the seed of democracy:

sprouts in the open air
of that soil
which is freely watered
by the freedom of expression
and where tongue of serpent
does not throw poison of fear
to fertilize the land
for the thorns of repression
to grow. (*Shrine* 61)

Offence cannot bring peace and harmony. It is a simple logic that they are unable to learn from the exile of Adam and Eve till now:

When Adam and Eve
broke the scepter of the divine law,
they were chased out from there;
only mother earth gave them refuge. (*Shrine* 36)

They have not learned lessons from their guilt but they are still cooled by their vices, fertilizing them on the soil of mother earth:

On the soil of her mind
they planted
the seed of the tree of knowledge
which they managed to steal.
It has yielded the fruit of
jealousy, superiority, murders
rapes and exploitation in abundance. (*Shrine* 36)

The poet does not talk about politicians particularly, but in general. Others are also responsible for disturbing peace and harmony, whether they belong to politics or religion or education or science. If they do not amend themselves, they:

will be soon exiled to another planet
as their ancestors were.
Where will they go from here
is a question now. (*Shrine* 37)

Gill holds a mirror to the masses to show what is stabbing at their back. He provokes to vent their furies that buried deep into their hearts. He mentions their sufferings in several poems. He says that the common people die in assaults whether it is of war, terrorism or riot and it happens in the whole world:

It is a familiar scene
from Bangladesh
at the time of freedom;
or a place in the middle-east,
Bosnia, Rwanda,
Somalia or Lebanon.
It may be any country in Asia
Africa, Europe or South America. (*Shrine* 71)

Besides, they are also exhausted of:

Heavy taxes
less service
higher unemployment
financial obligations
more elderly persons
soaring prices
increase in terrorism
shortage of physicians
violence on the street
no security (*Shrine* 89)

The mirror reflects that we are carved as a flower but

we have sprouted thorns and weeds beside us that pinch us:

Humans were created like flowers;
but they become intoxicated
with pride
and created
their own plastic roses and jasmines
without roots. (*Shrine* 34)

In order to get rid of all these thorns "of war, hatred and illusions" crowd needs "the caring arms of the earth" and "the soft nurse of nature / and a mysterious rain." But nature grants it only to those who are awakened. And they still sleep and wait:

...for a Hercules
for deliverance from vultures
who snatch the bread of peace
or a Minerva
who would help to bring down
the fire again. (*Shrine* 99)

Gill endeavors to arouse them from their sleep. Being awakened, they may say:

All the storms and tornadoes
and all the thunders
I can face alone. (*Shrine* 58)

Because:

...their leaders are unable to see
maddening clouds of dangers
and their rulers unable to hear
distressing cries of the innocent
though they are blessed
with sound ears and healthy eyes. (*Shrine* 147)

We accuse others for what is happening around us but we never peep into our heart or try to find how much responsible we are for that. Gill illustrates that most of our social problems emerge from our selfish and sinful nature. We help crime and criminals directly or indirectly. We do not even protest rather we watch only as a passive viewer. He mentions the present that asks to stand against the terror. "He leads the reader" says Michelle D. Cownell: "to believe it isn't up to governments, or wars or others to bring about peace; but that all of us can do our part" (194).

The 'citizens crave peace', justice, truth, security, harmony, democracy and calm. They want to be rescued from the cave of insecurity, terror, offence, violence, injustice, exploitation and cruelty. Gill shows them those causes about which they have not ruminated earlier. Now, they have come to know its roots and sources and they want to exile them from the universe.

According to Gill, a 'poem should not be predictable, and it should not be constructed on the trodden path' (Agarwal 115). Undoubtedly, he leads his readers into a world that is unknown to them. His poems deal with war, terrorism, peace, and other social concerns like AIDS. He moulds the sensibility of the readers about these social issues. Bianca Elliot commends Gill's ability of presentation:

> *I have never touched a person with AIDS. I never have spoken with a person who has suffered extreme neglect or persecution. The knowledge about these and other people like them exists but they are only on the news or in the paper. I don't "see" them. That changes a little when I read Shrine.* (Shrine 197)

Gill uses 'fresh language and images' which make 'stone stony.' His poems are 'candle that spreads the fragrance of light' and take his readers to higher level from where they can see everything crystal clear. Many poems of *Shrine* focus on the elements of evil of war and terrorism. He makes distinction between the world of terror and violence and the world of peace and harmony; he calls his readers into the world of peace and harmony.

References

Agarwal, N.K., ed., 'A Critique of Stephen Gill's Literary Sensibility.' *Discovering Stephen Gill: A Collection of Papers and Articles.* Delhi: Authorspress, 2008. 91-110.

——Stephen Gill On His Writing and Diaspora, *Discovering Stephen Gill: A Collection of Papers and Articles,* 111-132.

Connell, Michelle D., 'Gill's *Shrine* Implores to Think,' *Glimpses.* ed. Hamadan Darwesh. Ontario: Vesta, 2005. 194.

Elliot, Bianca. '*Shrine*' *Glimpses.* pp. 197-99.

Gill, Stephen. *Shrine.* Arizona: World University Press, 1999.

Khatri, C. L. "*Shrine*" (Poems of Social Concern) *Glimpses* pp. 188-89.

11

Vision and Commitment in the Poetry of Stephen Gill

Shujaat Hussain

Stephen Gill is a committed visionary and poet. His vision and commitment to the poetry is based on the universal values of truth, peace and love. The absence of these human values has created imbalance in the mind of man as well as the society. This imbalance in the society hints at another world war around the corner. Naturally, peace becomes the recurrent theme of Stephen Gill's poetry.

Stephen Gill has witnessed horror shortly before and after the partition of India. He records in Author's Preface of *Shrine:*

> *Humans were killed in the midst of a crowd because they happened to look different due to their dress or shaving pattern...In several cases, the stabbers could be friends, neighbours or anyone who knew the religion of the victims. Many made use of the lawlessness to settle old scores.* (*Shrine* 11)

He presents the scene as if he was running a commentary of the holocaust:

We froze inside of our house. The nights were nightmares and the days did not bring any hope. Often, the mornings dawned with more lamentable events. It was not easy to sleep when night after night the ghosts of fear looked straight into our eyes. Passers-by and neighbours appeared to be the possible killers. Apparently, the dark forces of religion roamed around freely to terrorize minorities. (11)

Stephen Gill adds:

I saw a crowd wearing helmets and chest braces and carrying swords, axes, spears and daggers, running in his direction. Some shouted that they saw a Muslim riding a bicycle over there. I could recognize some people. They were polite and humble ordinary shopkeepers and others. That afternoon they wore the mantle of crusaders. I had the feeling that the whole Christian family where the crowd headed was in trouble. (12)

It is painful to him when he says:

One can imagine the severity of his fear and also of his hosts when there were only two or three Christian families in that area and the crowd was not human in any case and Christians were only tolerated. (12)

In another scene he presents barbarity on the street of New Delhi:

One afternoon, the old man ran out of his house...Two or three pieces of rock hit him and he fell....A few people collected wood and kerosene oil from the neighbourhood, heaped them above and burnt his body.....The police officers passed the scene as if there was not even a fire. (13)

Gill records what he sees:

I cannot forget the pain and disgrace we had to go through for a crime we had not committed....There was nothing that we could do in any case...The only wise step that my parents had taken was to send my two elder sisters

> *to a convent because young females at home were harbingers of tragedy.* (15)

He says further that "The thought of cruelty of humans always remained in my mind like my own shadow. The more I thought of it, the more I became obsessed to write about it" (24). Stephen Gill who has witnessed human degradation, feels to shape his experiences in writing. A widely read and traveled Stephen Gill knows what humans have done to human. He is convinced that a human is his own enemy that is clear from the following lines from 'Image of Flowers':

Humans were created like flowers
but they became intoxicated
with pride
and created
their roses and jasmines
without roots (42)

Stephen Gill is hopeful because he talks of the roots that are essential for the existence of trees and plants to bear flowers and fruit:

Humans still need
the caring arms of the earth
because they are
flowers. (43)

'Garden of Eden', he says, was a distant planet where peace and prosperity prospered. When Adam and Eve broke the divine law they were thrown out and mother earth provided them refuge. Adam and Eve used their mind and planted the seed of knowledge. Now their generation is reaping:

It has yielded the fruit of

jealousy, superiority, murders,
rapes and exploitation in abundance. (44)

The blood of Cain is still on the earth. Earth could soak it, but the heat of the sun has failed to dry it up— dust is too weak to cover it. It has now poisoned the arteries of the mother. Stephen Gill asserts that Eve's children will be exiled to another planet but the question is where? Whatever he feels and witnesses, make him restless:

They are sure
to carry the seed of this tree
to corrupt the house of host
there also.(45)

Stephen Gill is against war, hatred and illusions. Imagery is the most powerful weapon in the literary armory of Stephen Gill. He uses it at right time so it yields desired outcome. He is quite aware of the violence. Much blood has been shed on the name of peace.

Human bones are its pillars constructed by the body. The power of Gill's pen demonstrates courage to defeat demons with his rhyme and wit.

'Flower of the Universe' another poem of Gill, portrays the same feeling of the poet. He presents truth through a flower because human is in the image of the flower:

Inside the stem
I saw a chaotic human crowd
under the darkening dust
of war, hatred and illusions.
....
the flower needed
the softness of nature
and mysterious rain. (46)

Another poem, 'Talking of Peace', is the result of the poet's experiences and beliefs. The fractured human lives, tainted love, pricking harmony, flawed fraternity and activities towards self-annihilation must have an impact on his vision. He makes readers feel his pulse and his insights that reach the places where wars are waged on the name of some pretext.

Stephen Gill is a poet who wants to see the welfare of human beings so that life on earth may acquire a higher potency and value. As poetry is life so no one can imagine poetry if there is no life, love, peace, faith, trusts, fraternity, humanity, happiness, and prosperity. Wars and bloodshed destroy them all. The result of their destruction is portrayed in 'War Fever'. The poet says that war brings darkness to the mind and spoils the truth of happiness and mutilates the body of humanity. It seizes sons from mothers and cultivates thorns. Those who suffer from war -fever worship violence:

War fever
kills the lamb of truth
drags into the vortex of hatred
causes a thirst for power
admires the roar of the cannon
and urges
crushing of peace. (54)

For Stephen Gill poetry is not to enjoy the love of beautiful women. He has no time to talk about the wine, lips, kisses, and speeches of national leaders. Neither has he time to talk about the melody of the nightingale of Keats, spontaneity of Wordsworth, delight of Frost and romance of Byron. For him, it is time to utter the truth, setting aside emotions, mundane glory, border disputes, religion, colour and creed. He is committed to write about the serious aspects of life relating to peace. One of his poems 'Talking of Peace' is a fine example, where he says:

Our rulers talk of peace
but it is futile
when nuclear-powered marines

sail over breasts of the oceans
missiles look down like hawks
and neutrons
make fun of every life. (52)

Peace cannot be achieved in the situations that have been created by so called politicians and leaders. *'Citizens are in the prison of fears'*, *'daily bread doled out by murderers'* , *'love worshipped with bullets'* , *'homes are destroyed'*, *'arteries of ignorance continue hardening'*, and *'merciless locusts of the basic needs keep buzzing over individuals'* (52). The poet is utmost bold and without the lust for accolades. In the last stanza of this poem 'Talking of Peace' he asks:

Now you tell me
My friend
How peace can come (53)

The answer easily controls the arms dealers and engines of destruction. This idea has been explored further in 'Arms Trader':

In the web of greed
arms traders forget the dove
hidden in the caves of blood. (55)

The poem 'The Gulf Crisis on TV' is along the same lines. Going over the poem with concentration without breaking rhythm generates a voice of pains and anxieties:

> *Once the financial Goliaths of their nations .... the moon of the moonless nights spreads the coffin of nightmares and the whirlwind of anarchy swept aside the faded flowers of their comforts for no fault of their own. The people of their own land watching the sinking sun of their hopes, without water, sanitation; medical relief and they were kept alive through the charity of two meals a day.* (58)

Women crying
around debris
men hurling abuses
children confused and despaired
the Patriots intercepting the Scuds
the showers of the bullets
downing the planes, and
the bombs piercing through homes
present a video game of Nintendo
or shots
from a festival of firecrackers. (59)

Stephen Gill appears to be tearful in his poem 'A Familiar Scene', which is enough to sink in grief to those who have engaged themselves in arms trade. Describing this heart-rending scene, he says:

> *people were chased to be cut down as if they were carrots', 'bodies rotting in ditches', 'bodies dumped with the garbage', 'bodies without hands', 'heads without bodies', 'who will tell whose young body is here'*, and *'who are these faces on whose eyes and cheeks drops of blood glitter like pearls.'*(70)

These lines portray the wail of a mother for her beloved. This familiar scene could be anywhere in Iraq, Afghanistan, Philistine, Sri Lanka, Bosnia, Rwanda, Asia, Africa, Europe and South America:

Here is a mother
who moves the corpses
to find her son;
here is the cry of an old man
buried in the cries of the wounded.
Who are these innocents
whom the storm of cruelty
has extinguished
as if they were candles. (71)

Stephen Gill protests against everything that stands in the way of his vision, regarding religious and national fanaticism. Religion preaches to shun the path of evils. Its first principle is to love humans and work for the welfare of all. Honesty, humanity, generosity and humility are the core of religion. When religion is misunderstood, it becomes dangerous. He presents this view in 'Religious Fanaticism':

It breeds
the daughters of fire
storm
sword and wound
the adders of dread
destruction
disdain
and distate. (66)

Stephen Gill condemns not only religious fanaticism, but also national fanaticism, because nationalism in narrow sense is also detrimental to world peace. The best example of national fanaticism is his poem 'Go Back'.

Citizens from time immemorial have been emigrating from one country to another, either to study or to be in a greener pasture. Sometimes, migration cannot be easy because of some kind of discrimination, even though migrants offer the boon of their life to their new found mother and the warmth of their blood to the snow. It is insensitive for the citizens of that country to raise voice to go back. It happens in this poem 'Go Back'. The poet answers the caller politely but in a bitter and biting way:

Open your eyes, my friend
in the clean air to see
that the world has become a village
where no one is an island to self
anymore
anymore. (81)

The poet hopes for someone to appear to cause radical changes. He suggests to wait for that day in his poem 'Children of Prometheus'.

Citizens wait for a Hercules
for deliverance from the vultures
who snatch the bread of peace
or a Minerva
who would help to bring down
the fire again. (92)

In another poem, 'Blind and Deaf', he believes that Moses and Christ will appear again to redeem the world:

I envision
Moses again coming down the hills
to see the crowd swayed
with a self-brewed wine
and Christ led to Calvery. (136)

Stephen Gill also talks about the citizens of the country where he was born:

> *I emphasized that it was a lack of tolerance that led to the division of India, and the division has made the situation worse. It was again lack of tolerance that led to the division of Pakistan and formation of Bangladesh. That has also made the situation worse. India needs tolerance, which was preached by the Buddha and again by Mahatma Gandhi. They preached tolerance because India always lacked it. India should follow these prophets of peace, otherwise there will be further fragmentation of the land.* (35)

Stephen Gill's poetry is marked by the virility of thought, decency of tone, precision of language, metrical versatility, and affectionate feelings. Many of his poems have different rhyme schemes, and variations of lines within stanzas. His individuality magnifies his stature as a poet among other poets. His poetry excels not only in formal beauty, but also in emotional colour. His creation has the fragrance that delights, soothes and provides comfort.

In the predominantly commercialized atmosphere of today, Stephen Gill works for the achievement of his vision with peace. His poetry is distinguished for a sweet simplicity, and a lyrical evocativeness that speaks of the eternal longings of the soul. Sometimes his imagery is complex yet fresh and photographic. As a poet of protest and a voice of liberty and angst, Stephen Gill enjoys a secure status in the pantheon of revolutionary poets. Because of these marked traits, his poetry can rightly be termed as Stephenian.

References

Stephen Gill, *Shrine* (rev. edn.), Published by Cyberwit.net, Allahabad, 2008. (All the references are from this book.)

12

Gill's Concern for Peace: A Critical Note

K.P. Singh

Stephen Gill, a multiple award-winning writer and versatile genius of our time writes exclusively on global peace and social concerns. For the last two decades he has chosen the path of a torch-bearer for humanity through poetry. His unique poetic prism has shown a powerful array of nuances that sheds light for peaceful co-existence. His message of peace through peaceful means can eliminate 'the withered leaves of greed' and the valley of 'terror' from the world. This harbinger of peace is having several emblems of peace, particularly the dove, in his poetry.

Stephen Gill is a poet, novelist, short story writer and literary critic from India, now settled in Canada. As a poet, he has raised his voice against the waves of violence in India and Pakistan during the 1947 Partition days. He has forcefully pleaded for peace and harmony in the war-torn world of today. In his poem 'Harmony' from *Songs Before Shrine*, he writes:

For the culture of dialogue
harmony weaves fabrics

for warmth
to womb the fetus of wisdom.
Harmony
the author of prosperities
composes a sonata
for the piano of delight. (SBS 19)

Dr. Rochelle L. Holt, a critic and poet from the United States of America writes:

> *While most are struggling in the Nineties to stress the differences of many cultures, Stephen Gill is professing the opposite, a more complex cognition which the masses have not yet learned in a yearning for separate glorification of each race, each colour, each sex, each age. We only enrich our culture by borrowing from all cultures, the poet has said. This makes any society more rational, more friendly, more peaceful, aiding in the eternal promotion of humanhood. (Glimpses* 160).

Gill strongly feels that there is a vast cultural gap between the East and West, and this cultural gap can be bridged by establishing harmony between them. When harmony is established a new world order will be created. In this world order, people will live with love and warmth, prosperity and delight. Poems on this message abound in *Songs Before Shrine.* Some of them are: 'Harmony and Peace', 'Evening of Harmony', 'Rays of Harmony', and 'When.' In reality, harmony and peace are the cardinal elements of his songs. Realizing the great need of peace in the present-day world, the poet utters aloud:

Wearing
a jacket of peace
let me swim to the shores
where freedom flow.
I would like to bathe in the waters
that spout from the fountain
of your comforting grace. (SBS 10)

No doubt, Gill is a great messenger of, even propagandist at times, of peace, which often he associates with such qualities as love and glory, comforts and prosperity, truth and beauty, delight and benediction. In the poem 'My Name is Peace', he says: "I am eternal / I am peace" (*SBS* 11). In the Preface of *Songs Before Shrine* Gill writes:

> *Poetry is to present my vision and my concerns, and to conceive peaceful way. The compelling influence for my crusade is the peace that is beauty; the peace that is creative; the peace that makes life meaningful. I attempt to illustrate that peace in its myriad forms on the rocks of my words. These rocks shout that Lazarus buried under them longs for life.* (xxi)

Gill lays emphasis on peace and harmony in order to erase insecurity and tension from the human world. He attempts to create a world-order in which the distracting question of dual identity or multiple identities does not arise. He repeats this way of thinking again and again. In the poem 'The Dove of Peace' in *Song Before Shrine* he says:

For a long time
I have been hearing
the dove of peace will be freed
shortly.
Progress has been made....
our homes now better adorned
with thorns of hatred
a few more nuclear bombs
remains to be developed
and contested
man has to breathe his last
in the smoke... (SBS 8)

Earlier in another poem 'Talking of Peace', he writes:

Our rulers talk of peace
but it is futile

when nuclear powered marines
sail over breasts of the oceans;
missiles look down like hawks
and neutrons
make fun of every life. (*Shrine* 52)

In many of his poems, the poet warns us against the horrors of war. War is destructive by nature. Moreover it cannot solve human problems. War can do harm but no good. Those people who believe that war is for 'winning glory'... 'boasting pride'... 'settling disputes' are really wrong. War is only a fraud and senseless killing. It makes women widows and children orphan. It makes many people maimed and handsome persons handless. It pollutes air and water. The innocents suffer most during and after war.

They are deprived of their basic needs, including food, shelter, sanitation and medicine. The places of worship are endangered. The poet says that the whole world will be destroyed completely, if a third world war breaks out. The world is in the teeth of destruction because of nuclear weapons. In the words of the poet, the people who fought in the war condemn it. The poet echoes the words of those people when he says: "war chokes the joy of life/ victor and loser suffer/ it kills man's hope / bringing destruction to all".

Thus the poet hates and condemns the war. He hopes for a world in which peace and harmony would reside. Gill believes that one of the major causes for disturbance of world peace and social harmony is religious fanaticism. The poet is of the view that citizens must fight against racism and bigotry to establish peace and harmony in the world.

Gill's poetry touches diverse topics including war, abuse, death and disease. He, however, always returns to the dove of peace, the god of harmony, the voice of oneness, and the rainbow strings. His art extends to a new vision of nobility and calls to gaze upon the face of hope and peace.

In his poem, 'The Flame', Gill prays for the deliverance from the ugly disharmony and terrorism. He prays to the divine:

To direct my steps
towards the shores of the pure bliss
of your peace
I shall dip in the esoteric stream
that meanders along the woodlands
of my absolute fidelity. (The Flame 62)

On the basis of experiences from the childhood to the present socio-politico- economic conditions of the world, Gill has become peace prone. He earnestly wishes to establish a peaceful world order. Dr. George Hines in his book *Stephen Gill & His works* remarks:

> *Dr. Gill's poetry shows the impact of World Federalism. His collections revolve around world unity and survival. "The United Nations" expresses his respect for the founding principles of the United Nations and his admiration for its efforts to foster peace and harmony in the world.*
>
> *Poems like "To War Mongers" and "War is Fraud" condemn war openly. There are references to war and to the unity of mankind in other poems.* (xvii)

Not only has he written poems urging for a world order but also has edited two volumes of anti-war anthologies of poems. "I hope that my writings about peace will cause change in the thinking of my readers", he has written.

Like the swan in Yeats' poetry, Gill's dominant image is dove, which stands for world peace. But the dove is under threat:

Sleeping / in the web of greed
arms traders forget the dove
hidden in the caves of blood. (Shrine 55)

The dove of peace lies in tatters. The dove is intimidated by the "hounds of war" and is smeared in blood:

The dove pleads
that the dance of the hounds

be stopped
to let her pacifying carol
fortify human muscles
to build more Taj Mahals
and pyramids of justice. (Shrine 60)

The poetry of Gill unravels the democratic vistas. He dreams of flowers of democracy blooming everywhere in the world. In the poem "My Beliefs", he makes his dream clear. He advocates that to attain that dream, mankind needs a democratic vision:

I rather believe
famine is man-made
and sunshine a child of peace. (Shrine 146)

Stephen Gill is totally against the sword, the bullet and the bomb. He had a surfeit of weapons in his childhood, which are soaked in blood.

Those who kiss
the lips of the sword
fall victims to its fury. (Shrine 145)

The rise of fundamentalism and the despotic rules and the walls of mistrust fill him with anguish:

I am a human
I love humankind.
Smile, my friend
because
we are all one. (SBS 61)

The poetry of Gill summons us to the threshold of peace, and the river of imagination. He believes in unconditional love and global peace through a democratically elected world government. He is certainly a citizen of the world, a trait that is obvious from his poems.

His poem 'To Be' sums up in a few lines his poetic credo:

The muse
that muscles the vision of poets
shape my pen into plough
that will prepare my land
for sowing peace
wherever its blade touches. (*SBS* 2)

Gill's poetry reminds us of Eliot's message conveyed in the *Waste Land* where he wishes *Shanti* to come to this world which has been made a desert by the lack of moral values. Eliot writes in his famous poem *The Waste Land*:

These fragments I have shored against my ruins
Why then Ile fit you. Hieronymo's mad againe.
Datta. Dayadhvam. Damyata.
Shantih Shantih Shantih (90)

Eliot is of the opinion that Sanskrit word *Shanti* signifies 'the peace which passes understanding' and is meaningful repetition of the known ending of the great Upanishads.

In Gill's case the world is in a state of crisis due to lack of harmony. Both the poets pray for peace. Attainment of 'Shanti' is the poetic goal of them. Gill wishes to establish the kingdom of peace in the world, while Eliot gropes and finds *Shanti* or peace within one's self. Real peace is not somewhere out, it is our very nature, so once a man balances and attains peace inwardly, whatever he acts or omits, results in peace. However Gill emphasizes more on outer peace remaining a bit indifferent to Eliot's assumption, he has to develop and motivate his readers to seek the same peace within their own heart so that inner exploration of peace may be sounder and even lasting.

References

Darwesh, Hamadan. *Glimpses*, Vesta (Canada), 2005.

Eliot, T.S., *The Waste Land*, New Delhi: OUP, 2001.

Gill, Stephen, *Shrine,* Arizona: World University Press, 1999.

——*Songs Before Shrine*. New Delhi: Authorspress, 2007. (Abbreviated as *SBS* in the text.)

Hines, George, *Stephen Gill & His Works,* New Delhi: Authorspress, 2008.

13

Symbolism with a Special Reference to My Poetry

Stephen Gill

The accurate representation of the feelings, thoughts, moods, sights, ideas and a variety of emotions is a serious enigma which poets face. Their representations are about personal opinions that are in the mind. Without going into philosophical or logical depth, I call them the god within. Language is inadequate to bring out the god within, because this god is intangible. In addition to a mastery over the language, communicators need special skills and movements of hands, raising of eyebrows, changing tones, shrugging of shoulders and other gestures. Still, communications are not fully accurate and are likely to be misunderstood. Verbosity does not help either. Communication becomes more difficult in poetry because it is a form of condensed expression.

Therefore, poets use symbols to represent the god within at a higher level and also to add beauty. They take the help of metaphors to represent the god within. Aristotle said that metaphor is the soul of poetry. Metaphor is a figure of speech that is used for implied comparison. I have used this device freely in my poetry, such as "sickles of bigotry,"[1] ; "pilots of words"[2] ; "snakes of personal migraines"[3], "the albatross of intolerance"[4] ; and "a pyramid of justice"[5] to quote a few.

Symbol, a higher form of metaphor, comes from the Greek word sumbolon that means sign, mark and token. In Greek sumballein means to put together. Synonyms of symbolism include typology, metaphor and analogy. Symbolic poetry is visible expression of something that is invisible— a marriage between abstraction and concrete.

This device is used to express the hidden meaning veiled by the obvious meaning — to express something that is abstract as tangible. This device is also used to express something that is tangible in another tangible way.

Poetry is not a set of general statements. It is not verbosity either. It is a short cut to convey the message. The poetry that is symbolic may have several layers of meaning that is like peeling off the layers of an onion. It is also something like music that produces a mood. A poet may pick up colors for non-verbal communication that goes beyond ink. A skilled designer of a logo or website would be careful to select colors because they have impact on the mind and eye. He may keep in view that the impact of colors differs from culture to culture.

Words and punctuation marks as well as traffic signs, such as red lights that mean to stop, are some examples of obvious symbols. A red rose, a traditional symbol, signifies love and fidelity. Among other traditional symbols, a cross signifies a follower of Christ and the sunrise, a new beginning. The picture of scales is often used to represent justice. Traditionally, a lion represents bravery, a dove represents peace and purity, and the water, life. The symbol of winter or snow suggests aging and decay.

Creative artists also develop new, individual or personal symbols, mainly because they do not want to use cliché or trite expressions. Some of these individual symbols may pose problems for readers. To understand them, a reader may have to go over the poem more than once with close attention.

I have presented several of my poems in this vein. I often use the wind in various forms to symbolize my god within. Among several, I would like to select "To a Dove"[6] that appears on pages 132-33 and "Flight of a Dove"[7] on pages

134-35 of the Revised Edition of *Shrine*. I do not want to dissect them because dissection mars the beauty. Here is one quote:

I am
often greeted by the bursting flutters
of my dove
while rambling the rayless resort
of the fears
from the scamps of my surrounding.[7]

Another poem, "Unfair Ophelia", is from *Songs Before Shrine.*[8] Ophelia is a character from Hamlet by Shakespeare. Or take the case of "My Muse" on page 45 of the same collection:

Today
the jealous winds outside
smite my windows desperately
like a being insane
while inside I am at peace
with her.[9]

An example of non-traditional symbols appears in the first canto of *The Flame* which is the longest poem on modern terrorism in English. In the Preface of *The Flame*, and also elsewhere, I call my poems robins and explain how I care and nourish them.[10]

Trees and forests have appeared in different cultures as symbols. The oak has been used to signify strength, and maple to signify balance and promise. I have taken the assistance of several objects from nature to use this device. Tree is one of them. When I read my poetry objectively or as a critic after publication, I find that forests and trees have appeared often, such as "Maple trees of compassion"[11] ; and "tree of your amazement"[12]. From *Shrine*, my collection before *The Flame*, the notable lines are: "the dignity of the palm tree"[13] ; "the sobriety of the jungles"[14] ; "pineapples of happiness"[15] ; "the jungles of thoughts"[16] ; "the maple leaf of freedoms"[17] ; "gangers grow a jungle of night"[18] and the list can go on.

In the first line of canto fifteen of my longest poem, *The Flame* "The battered body of the abode/ of my flame /flaring in the dark..."[19] builds up a picture of the night that is dark. The night suggests loneliness and symbolizes several aspects associated with darkness. *The Flame* is presented as a human who has been murdered brutally and its parts severed. The mention of the battered body is to conjure up horrific emotion in the reader. The whole scene suggests fear, brutality and the darkness in the soul.

Symbolic devices provide oxygen to poetry. Symbolism becomes also a sort of double talk, not as strutting in a confused way.

It is not a talk like that of a drunk person or the distorted vision of a myopic. It is a deliberate attempt to say something other than what it literally means. For illustration, here is a poem "The Meech Lake Fish"[20] from *Songs Before Shrine,* where words like crocodiles, fish, bathers, banks, and waters present a scene of the sea to express another story associated with the Meech Lake Accord, an important part of Canadian political history. This Accord was signed by ten premiers and the prime minister in 1987. The Meech Lake Accord divided Canada badly in the 1980s.

To express the inexpressible, the god within, symbolists usually select objects from nature, usually flowers and oceans. These objects become symbols, because they are suggestive of something else. Through this device, a poet makes the god within, tangible. My poem "The Match Lake Fish", is an example.

Symbolists also refer to a major literary movement of the second half of the 19th century from France. The movement has received different labels, including decadence, aesticism, neoromanticism and imaginism. Its followers include Mallarme, Verlaine, and Rimbaud. Their main aim was to represent ideas and emotions by suggestion rather than description. They reacted against the prevailing school of realism and impressionism that expressed emotions or abstractions without comparing them with the visible world. Symbolists influenced painting and music as well as English writers like Poe, Swinburne and W.B. Yeats. Symbolists wrote in a highly suggestive way to express the intangible truth or conditions. They became more evocative than descriptive.

Nevertheless, the literary experiments of Symbolism cannot be dismissed. Among these, the most important is free verse, which resulted from a long process of dissolution of traditional forms and has now become an important department of poetry. The attacks the Symbolists faced were often undeserved. There existed indeed a "fin de Siecle" or decadent" affectation and a foggy or atmospheric type of art that were identified by some with Symbolism; but at no time since the Renaissance have so many experiments been carried out on the poetic values of words, and no school of poetry has so much enriched the technical means of poets."[21]

Though the Symbolist Movement in literature refers to poets in the later part of the nineteenth century, it has its precursors in several religious scriptures. Symbolic literature is old and easily traceable from the time of Plato in 400 BC. During these years, the literature of western Europe was dominated by symbols to understand God and for proper conduct. *Indian* epics such as the *Ramayana* and other books are full of symbolic features. Sufi poetry is usually symbolic because it uses worldly terminology to express divinity.

Although it is hard to pinpoint when the symbolist movement started in the history of literature, it was, actually, Jean More'as's article, published on 18 September, 1886, in Le Figaro, which made the literary world conscious of a new trend already developing in France. Many attempts by different writers were made to trace the uniform factors in the writings of the symbolists, but they failed.

In spite of their differences, the Symbolists were unanimous in calling Charles Baudelaire (1821-67), their precursor. His poetry is neither philosophizing nor didactic. The Symbolists appreciated Baudelaire's theory of "correspondences between the senses". The same theory was applied by Rimbaud in his sonnets. Rimbaud, like Gill, showed extraordinary interest in the use of neologism in his poetry. It is Mallarme (1842-98), who brought sym-bolist poetry to its near perfection. His *Divagations* (1897) is an important document for the symbolists. His Tuesday gatherings influenced many younger artists who attended them. Mallarme's poetry is an example of elusiveness. A rhythm or tone suggests the whole atmosphere. He prefers to use suggestive language and words in their etymological sense. As a result, his symbolism has become more private and obscure. Like Verlaine, he considers music to be of fundamental importance in poetry. His disciples Paul Valery who knew him personally, and Wallace Stevens, carried on his tradition. Wallace Stevens, an American, adapted his master's technique to the general vein of his country's atmosphere and temperament. Paul Verlaine (1844-96), another symbolist and also a lyrical poet, had no theory on art to offer. He scoffed at epithets like symbol-ist and decadent. But regarding technique he had de-finite views which he expressed in "Art Poetique" (1874).

Like Mallarme' he believed that poems should be musical. He preferred ambiguity to precision and a language suggestive rather than descriptive.

The Symbolists reacted against the poetry of that time, the Realist theatre and the Naturalist novel in order to express with the aid of symbols the mystery of existence.

The movement was started in France and a large part of those who were involved in it were artists of French origin. Paris, being a centre of art, attracted many young writers from different parts of the globe. When these writers returned to their respective countries they carried with them the symbolists' ideas. This helped in spreading this movement to the rest of the world. Among the followers of the symbolists only Jules Laforgue, Gustave Kahn, Rene Ghil and Albert Samin were French. From England there were Arthur Symons, W.B. Yeats and George Moore; from Germany, Rilke and Hauptmann; from Belgium, Maurice Maeterlinck; from Greece, Jean More'as, who wrote the symbolists' manifesto; from

America, Francis Viele' Griffin and Stuart Merrill; from Italy-D'Annunzio; and the Machado brothers from Spain.

The Symbolists avoided political and public themes in their works. They rejected society and ceased to be the official voices of their country. Therefore, with symbolism, art ceased in truth to be national and assumed the collective premises of Western culture. Its overwhelming concern was the non-temporal, non-sectarian, non-geographic and non-national problem of the human condition.[22]

In France, men of letters were often public figures, and literature, to a great extent, remained a part of public life—just the opposite of the normal practice in England. One of the chief factors which gave impetus to this new movement of symbolism was the complete estrangement of certain poets from the tone and attitude of public life around them. G.S. Fraser believes in fact the traditional values of much French literature—values of clear, rapid, sometimes superficial reasoning, of incisive generalization, of dignified rhetoric, and pointed wit, while real virtues in themselves were, as Baudelaire noted, anti-poetic virtues.[23] The Symbolists gave art the status of religion—it became mysterious with its own distinct language differ-ent from that of prose. The artists became completely isolated from the general public and their art also became vaguer. They revised their works repeatedlyand thoughtfully, and so made them more and more difficult for an average reader to understand.

This is the reason why even years after its publication, *Ulysses*, a novel, is read only by a microscopic minority of the intelligentsia. The Symbolists, who attempted to bring art and life together, did not usher in a new simplicity and clarity, but rather a new confusion.

Their master, Mallarme, himself is a difficult poet. Rimbaud is also obscure. "He speaks in a trance like an inspired drunkard."[24]

The Symbolists revolted against Parnassian poetry, yet, retained some of its concepts such as 'art for art's sake' and insistence on technical perfection. They scoffed at the scientific view of art as it was preached by Zola and Maupassant. They attempted chiefly to use a language that was suggestive and evocative rather than informative. They emphasized the careful selection of words, colours, tones, rhythms and phrases. Connotations became more important than simple denotations. Even denotations in their hands became tangled and vague. In art they became impersonal and believed in control. They employed the techniques of music in their art, for they believed that by its nature music reaches a deeper level of the unconscious. They learnt a good deal from the musical techniques of Wagnerian drama. Mallarme and Verlaine considered the musical elements in poetry to be of fundamental importance.

More'as claims that Symbolism is a reaction of the soul in literature against all those literary movements which represent things that only visibly exist, exactly as they exist. It is, he says, a reaction against a type of language that says rather than suggests. Symbolism, in practice, would free literature from the bondage of rhetoric, externals, regular beat in poetry, from the cataloguing of nature and the chance accidents of daily life, freeing the literary arts of all elements of materialism, which hitherto have prevented the dis-engagement of the ultimate essence of soul from its insignificant externals."[25]

In the theatrical world presentation of symbolism posed problems. But Antoine's production of Ibsen revealed the possibilities of symbol on stage. Ibsen also influenced directly some English dramatists. Like Ibsen, the English dramatists combined symbolism with naturalism. Apart from Ibsen's plays, Villiers de l'Isle - Adam's Axel was staged and Maeterlinck wrote wonderful plays suffused with a dream-like atmosphere. Alfred Jarry's highly satirical Ubu Roi (1896) caused an uproar.

The Symbolists did not make much contribution to fiction. Eduard Dujardin, a minor writer, influenced James Joyce. George Moore was friendly with Joyce. On his return to England, Joyce talked of Dujardin's technique which prompted him to read We'll to the Woods No More. He learnt from this novel Dujardin's technique of the stream-of-consciousness which he employed very successfully in Ulysses. Moore himself, who had started his literary career in the naturalistic tradition, gave it up in favour of symbolist techniques.

Whereas the previous writers deliberately emphasized their symbols, the modern symbolists simply give the symbols and leave the rest to the imagination of the readers. They want the symbols themselves to speak. Also, their symbols form part of the whole structure of their work. To understand a novel, a play or a poem, it is very important to realize first the significance of the symbols used in it. Karl and Magalaner elaborate the difference between the traditional and the modern use of symbols:

The difference between the two is one of emphasis, and in that area we have, perhaps, the chief difference between the traditional use of the symbol and the twentieth-century application. In that area, we can ascertain one of the difficulties the modern reader has when he comes to *A Portrait*, or *Ulysses, Mrs. Dolloway, The Waves, Women in Love, Nostromo,* etc., without any awareness that these novels will proceed differently from the ones he is probably accustomed to. More carefully arranged novels, he comes to realize, need more careful readers. The modern novelist often merely gives the materials and lets his symbols and other devices suggest whatever the reader can make of them. Furthermore, his symbols themselves will not always be clear—they may be in many different forms: short incidents, casual images, broken conversations, minor characters, peripheral scenes. And as the now list gains in imaginative power and maturity, he refines his symbols and makes their importance more subtly provoking. For the novelist realizes that as new areas of knowledge open, new symbols are needed for expression; so the reader must be on close guard or a major theme or motif may be lost; and in novels like *Nostromo, A Portrait, Ulysses, Point Counter Point,* and *A Passage to India,* which proceed by motifs and recurrent themes, one loses entire sequences if he is not completely alert to what the novelist is doing.[26]

Often a distinction is made between allegorical and

symbolist writings. Freud's analysis shows that no symbol can be interpreted in one way. The literary figures agree with Freud on the point that symbols cannot be tied down to a single meaning. On the other hand, an allegory has only single possible interpretation. To use Mr. Lain Fletcher's distinction between allegorical and symbolical poetry, if a poem is allegorical, 'it works out the details of something already given, something which has received prior justification as theology or political theory, an organization of intuitions and judgments. Valuation of this will depend on the structure of the poem, its music, its detail. With the poetry of symbol none of these things is of the first importance. A symbol has been defined as the expression of some otherwise inexpressible truth; and it is not on the verbal music, or on the in-cidental illustrations of the theme, that judgment will depend, but on the insight which the poem accords into the life of the soul.[27]

Arthur Symons, a poet-critic and also a prominent member of the Rhymers Club, holds an important position in the realm of modern English Literature. During his stay in France he regularly attended Mallarme's Tuesday gatherings. On coming back to Eng-land he put down what he had heard at those meetings in the form of criticism, evaluation and translation, in his book The Symbolist Movement in Literature (1899), dedicated to W.B. Yeats. The same year another book connected with symbolism, Freud's *Interpretation of Dreams,* appeared in Vienna. Although unlike in method, both recorded the search for a psychic reality which had little to do with exterior reality. Symons' book, like Freud's, gave a name to the preoccupation with modes of half-uttered or half-glimpsed meaning which, as we can see clearly enough now sixty years have passed, was a principal direction in modern thought.[28]

Symons' book acquainted the English people with new literary developments in France. His essays on Mallarme', Rimbaud, Verlaine, Huysman, Villiers de OIsle-Adam and Laforgue are better than the sketchy work of George Moore.

For Yeats, a new vista of imagination was opened through

the writings of these French writers. Villiers de l'Isle Adam's "Axel became Yeats' guide and beacon in his theory and practice of a dramatic art where symbol replaces characters, events are allegories and words keep more than half their secrets to themselves."[29] Yeats employed symbolism, as it is generally believed, for the same purpose for which Baudelaire put on the mask of a dandy. About Yeats as well as Baudelaire and his successors, it would be better "to speak of a Philistine City with the poets moving about it as spies, wearing a disguise, and communicating by a code that made their presence unsuspected.[30]

Yet it should be remembered that Yeats was not being freshly introduced to the nature and func-tion of the literary symbol of his new contacts; his study of magic, his work on Blake, and his natural literary inclination had already brought symbols into his early works. The Wanderings of Oisin is sufficient evidence. In a letter to Katherine Tynan, written towards the end of 1888, he spoke of the poem as saying several things under disguise of Symbolism.[31]

Among Indian poets, *Gitanjali* of Tagore stands out in the gallery of symbolists. The name of W.B. Yeats conjures up with Tagore. W.B. Yeats, an aristocrat by birth, was a good friend of Rabindanath Tagore, another aristocrat by birth. Yeats blue-penciled Tagore's *Gitanjali* and also nominated him for the Nobel Prize. Yeats was already a Nobel Laureate when he nominated Tagore. Yeats was a great admirer of Charles Baudelaire as a symbolist. The poems that greatly mirror the influence of the Symbolists, include Yeats's two Byzantium poems and the second coming. He used the devices of symbolism most favourably to make his poetry rich, elegant and communicative at a higher level.

Whereas W.B. Yeats wrote partly under the influence of the French Symbolist Movement, Rabindranath Tagore wrote *Gitanjali* under the influence of the centuries-old tradition of India. He makes use of the images of the flute, harp, flowers, fire, empty vessel and journey in the Indian tradition to represent his inexpressible devotion. I believe that personalities are shaped by the hands of the environment as pots are shaped by the hands of potters Yeats was shaped to a great extent by the French symbolists and Tagore by the early religious poetry of India. It is difficult for me to trace one single hand that shaped the art of my poetry. I can say that I cannot get away from the New Delhi of my early days, though I left India decades ago. In one way or the other, the well of New Delhi keeps providing water of creativity to my pen. I can also say that my poetry does not emerge at the annual festivals of poets. It does not emerge either at the releases of collections by publishers and celebrities nor does it emerge at the podiums. My poetry emerges gracefully when I trim off fat from the body of my muse, and knock off the wretched redundancies, freeing her from the pollutants of overused expressions. I feel better off after my faithful experimentations with imageries in the laboratory of linguistic surgery. This brings my poetry closer to the school of the symbolists than to any other school.

References

1. Stephen Gill, *Shrine*. India: Cyberwit.net, 2008, p. 78.
2. Stephen Gill, *Songs Before Shrine*. India: authorspress, New Delhi, 2007, p. 77.
3. Gill. op.cit., p. 114.
4. Stephen Gill, *The Flame*. Canada: Vesta Publicaitons, 2008, p. 106.
5. Stephen Gill, p. 98.
6. Stephen Gill, *Shrine*. India: Cyberwit.net, 2008, pp. 132-33.
7. Stephen Gill, pp. 134-135.
8. Stephen Gill, *Songs Before Shrine*. India: authorspress, New Delhi, 2007, pp. 29-30.
9. Stephen Gill, p. 45.
10. Stephen Gill, *The Flame*. Canada: Vesta Publicaitons, 2008, p. 7.
11. Stephen Gill, p. 41.
12. Stephen Gill, p. 48.

13. Stephen Gill, *Shrine*. India: Cyberwit.net, 2008, p. 41.
14. Stephen Gill, pp. 41 163…Essays on the Poetry of Stephen Gill.
15. Stephen Gill, p. 44.
16. Stephen Gill, p. 46.
17. Stephen Gill, p. 55.
18. Stephen Gill, 93.
19. Stephen Gill, *The Flame*, Canada: Vesta Publications, 2008, p. 59.
20. Stephen Gill, *Songs Before Shrine*. India: authorspress, New Delhi, 2007, p. 22.
21. *Collier's Encyclopedia*, Toronto, Canada, vol. 21.
22. Anna, Balakian, *The Symbolist Movement*. USA: Random House, New York, 1967, p. 10.
23. G.S. Fraser, *The Modern Writer and His World*. England: Pelican Books, 1967, p. 35.
24. G.S. Fraser, p. 42.
25. Karl, Frederick R. & Magalaner, Marvin. *A Readers Guide to Great Twentieth-Century* English Novels. USA, New York: The Noonday Press, 1964, p. 18.
26. Joseph Hone. *W.B. Yeats*. London: Macmillan & Co. Ltd. 1942, p. 156.
27. G.S. Fraser, *The Modern Writer and His World* England: Pelican Books, 1967, p. 37.
28. Arthur Symons. *The Symbolist Movement in Literature*. New York: E.P. Dutton & Co., 1958, p. vii.
29. Joseph Hone. *W.B. Yeats*, London: Macmillan & Co. Ltd. 1942, p. 106.
30. Fraser, G.S. *The Modern Writer and His World*, England: Pelican Books, 1967, p. 36.
31. Leonard E. Nathan, *The Tragic Drama of William Butler Yeats*. New York & London: Columbia University Press, 1965, p. 51.

14

Interview: Stephen Gill with A. K. Choudhary

Q. *Why do you write?*

A. To live. I use words to reincarnate myself to live peacefully in my home that is poetry.

Q. How do you define a good poem?

A. A good poem will touch my soul, and a poem will touch my soul if it follows the rules of craftsmanship that includes the use of imagery, language, and fresh phrases. Fat and over-used expressions are the pesticides that irritate me. A good poem is mostly bones and muscles.

Q. How has your writing been received?

A. Reasonably well.

Q. What is your masterpiece?

A. A mother loves all her children equally. However, I am pleased especially with *Shrine,* a collection of poems about peace and social concerns. I am equally pleased with *The Flame,* the longest poem in English on modern terrorism, is about the destruction caused by maniac messiahs.

In fiction, I am pleased with *Immigrant,* a novel about the hopes and fears and struggles of a newcomer from India to Canada. The novel is also about the perception of people

* First published in *Kohinoor* (India), No. 2, Vol. 4, June 2008, pp. 1-10

from Indian continent about Canada. It is also about the perception of Canadians about that continent. I have tried to tear off the curtain of ignorance in the novel. I believe that discrimination is largely the child of ignorance.

Q. Will you please tell us something about your childhood memories? How was your parentage and bringing up?

A. For years, I avoided discussions about my childhood, because it has always been unpleasant to resurrect those unhappy days in the lap of Delhi. I have talked about those unhappy days now in the prefaces of my collections of poems. My preface to *Shrine* (poems), *Songs Before Shrine* (poems), and also *The Flame* have enough glimpses of my childhood

Q. Were those conditions conducive to flower your genius?

A. Conducive conditions have been interludes in my life to catch fresh air. Whenever I fell down struck by the blows from the persistent conditions of suffocation, I rose with more determination and vigour to walk towards my horizon. A traveler has to cover some distance everyday to proceed towards his or her horizon. In the end, it is not the end that matters, it is the journey that matters the most. Relentlessness is the mantra of my life.

Q. Are you a satisfied person vis-a-vis your literary and academic pursuits?

A. Academic pursuits are not helpful to the person who wants to settle down as a writer. To be satisfied in the literary field is something else. Satisfaction is the fulfilment of needs or expectations. Satisfaction largely depends on a person's expectations. If the expectations are at their zenith, they are not easily achievable.

I always wanted to be a poet and writer. A poet is the candle that burns itself in order to give light. It is a struggle to be a meaningful poet and this struggle never ends because it is a never-ending journey for a horizon that is non-achievable. No serious writer can say that he or she is fully satisfied with his or her writings. I am satisfied to be a writer and poet and dissatisfied at the same time because I have not been able to touch the shores of my horizon. I am still yearning to ride its waves which I see bathing in the golden rays of the sun.

Q. Which of your poems / stories are specifically autobiographical in nature?

A. In a way, most poems and fiction are autobiographical, because they present views and sometimes segments from life of their creator. These views may be based on facts, real experiences, ideas or events in the life of the artist. That is why no two artists say the same, though the objects or events may be the same. One example is the nightingale. Several poets have been inspired by the same bird but in different ways. The object is the same but when a poet writes about his or her experience, it comes out differently from the smithy of the self, where the object goes through the process of transformation. Because every poem tells something about its creator, it is autobiographical in some ways.

However, some poems and fiction are more autobiographical than the others. I will include my last poem, called "autobiography" in *Shrine,* as well as "Go back" and several other pieces in the category of autobiographical poems. They are not straight autobiographies. On the other hand, my prefaces to the collections of my poems are based on straight personal information.

In my novel *Immigrant* I have borrowed considerably from my personal life. But this novel is not an autobiography. There is a vast difference between an autobiography and autobiographical elements. It may confuse the reader who attempts to trace autobiographical elements in a piece of art. Such attempts do not serve any serious purpose.

Q. What are the themes of your writings?

A. Peace and social concerns.

Q. As a writer, to which tradition do you see yourself belonging?

A. None. I am establishing my own tradition. If there is any, I will leave this to critics to find out.

Q. Do you want to give any message for our readers?

A. Readers should find out what they want, though it is not that easy. Some are destined to do certain things that are clear to them from their early life. Those who do not know, should sit down and meditate to find an answer. If they do not come up with any answer, they should not condemn themselves. They may be destined to help others or raise a family in a graceful way. This is a serious and meaningful destiny. Whatever a person wants to do, he or she should do it with the whole mind, soul and devotion. There are no short cuts.

Those who want to serve the muse should not compete with their neighbours and friends, or with anyone. My message to them is to compete with their horizon. They should believe in giving. Giving is not waste—it is sharing. There is much wisdom in the wise words of the wisest soul that ever walked on earth, "Give and it shall be given to you." It applies in the realm of writing in the form of advice, sharing marketing knowledge and helping in any way possible.

Always find time to worship the muse. Those who wait for the better times will not be able to serve the muse. Every human needs daily food. No one can take the food of the whole month in a day. In the same way, the ration of daily consumption has to be consumed daily. It can be less or nominal, but it should be there. Writers should find time everyday to be able to write on the project they have in mind. The gist of my message is write, write, write, and get published.

To get published, they should start first with their local newspapers, magazines and newsletters. They should join groups of writers and if there is none, form one. Problems about writing, including where and how to get published, are some topics to discuss in these gatherings. India has some good poets of English. Invite them to your meetings for discussions.

Also, develop the habit of reading articles and books on writing. Local libraries should have books on such subjects. If they do not, ask librarians to stock such books. Also read good poetry and analyze it to find out why that poetry is considered good.

Do not force anyone to publish your work when the

editor or publisher does not think it is worth publishing. A good poem or fiction will eventually find a market. If one editor rejects it, send it to another. Meanwhile, keep polishing and improving the work. Those who want to get published abroad should start with the local market. Do not ask your friends abroad to send your material to a publisher for you. It does not work in the

West, as it does in India. Such writers or would-be writers lose both— their friends and also time. Serious writers and readers should focus first on their writing to improve it. You may ask your friends to give you the names and addresses of the possible editors, publications and publishers who may consider publishing your type of work. The next step for you is to get in touch directly with those outlets. Do not expect your friends to do this work for you. It would show that you are naive and no one would like to publish a work by naive writers.

For additional guidance, I would advise readers to read my prefaces to the collections of my poems. I have discussed different aspects of writing in these prefaces. I will also advise them to visit my web site (www.stephengill.ca) and read "*Stephen Gill on poetry and poets,*" listed to the left in the side bar.

Q. Give details of your publications.

A. Here are details:

POETRY

* *Shrine* (World University Press), poems, 1999

* *Songs Before Shrine* (authorspress) collection of the following four collections of poems:

—1. *Reflections & Wounds* (poems) Hc. Vesta, 1978

—2. *The Dove of Peace* (poems) Pb., MAF Press, NY 1989, 1993

—3 *Songs for Harmony* (poems) Pb., Rose Shell Press, NJ, 1993

—4.*Divergent Shades* (poems) Xavier's College, India 1995

* *Flashes* (trilliums in haiku spirit), Imprint
* *The Flame* (Vesta) This is the longest poem ever written in English on modern terrorism.

FICTION

* *Life's Vagaries* (short stories)
* *The Loyalist City* (a novel)
* *Why* (a novel)
* *Immigrant* (a novel)
* *Simon & the Snow King* (children story, Illust.)
* *The Blessings of a Bird* (children story, illust)

CRITICAL STUDIES

* Scientific Romances of H.G. Wells

* *Six Symbolist Plays of Yeats*
* Political Convictions of G.B. Shaw

MISCELLENOUS

* *The Discovery of Bangladesh* (history)
* *Sketches of India* (illust. essays about India)
* *English Grammar for Beginners*

BOOKS IN URDU, PANJABI AND HINDI

* *Aman Di Ghuggi* (Poems in Panjabi language)
* *Jazeera* (poems in Urdu)
* *Jazeera* (poems in Hindi)

BOOKS EDITED

* *Poets of the Capital* (Ottawa poets)
* *Seaway Valley Poets*
* *Tales from Canada for Children Everywhere*
* *Green Snow: Anthology of Canadian Poets of Asian Origin*
* *Anti-War Poems*: Vol. 1
* *Anti-War Poems*: Vol. 2
* *Vesta's Who's Who of North American Poets* (Vesta 1990)

WORKS IN TRANSLATION

-*Zakhmi Perchawen* (poems in Punjabi). Translator: Dr. Mohinder Kaur Gill. Hc., Suchinton Prakashan, New Delhi, India, 1980

-*Awasi* (Punjabi translation of his novel *Immigrant).* Translator: Balbir Momi. Pb., Pal Pocket Books, Amritsar, India, 1986.

-*Parwasi* (translation of *IMMIGRANT* in Panjabi) Translators: Dr. N. Singh and S. Sarna. Pb., 1989. Vikendrit Group of Publications, Delhi, India.

-*Reflexions Et Blessures* (poems in French). Translator: Fr. Roland Hamel, Vesta, 1979.

ADDITIONAL INFORMATION

My poetry and prose have appeared in more than five hundred publications, mostly in Canada, the United States and India. I have also written and published book reviews, research papers on writers from the East and the West, and articles on world peace. I have also written poetry in Urdu, Hindi and Punjabi. Some of my Urdu/Hindi poems have been put to music and performed by prominent singers. Those songs have been released in two CD's, titled *AMAN,* and another CD is titled *AMAN KI RAH.*

I would like to share further that I receive doctoral dissertations regularly from universities for evaluation. Scholars at some universities are doing research at doctoral levels on my books.

Four Books of critical studies are available on my works:

1. *Glimpses* (published articles and research papers). Ed. Hamadan Derwesh, Vesta, Canada
2. *Stephen Gill and His Works* by Dr. George Hines, Authorspress, New Delhi
3. *Discovering Stephen Gill* (unpublished research papers and articles). Ed. Dr. Nilanshu K. Agarwal, Authorspress.

4. *The Flame Unmasked* Ed. Dr Sudhir K. Arora, Prakash Books Depot.

There is also a DVD of my interviews on television. This DVD is called *INTERVIEWS WITH DR. STEPHEN GILL.* I have discussed my books, art of writing and my message about peace in these interviews.

NOTE: Stephen Gill will be pleased to send complimentary copies of his collections of poems and novel *Immigrant* to those who would like to write research papers.

CONTACT: stephengill@cogeco.ca

Select Bibliography

Poetry

Gill, Stephen. *Reflections.* Kites, 1973.

........*Wounds.* Vesta, 1974

.......*Moans and Waves.* Vesta, 1989.

.......*The Flowers of Thirst.* Vesta, 1991.

.......*The Dove of Peace.* M. F. Press, 1993.

......*Songs For Harmony.* Rose Shell Press, 1993.

.......*Divergent Shades.* Writer's Forum, 1995.

Shrine. (First published by World University Press, 1999). Rev. Ed. Cyberwit, Allahabad, 2008.

Flashes. (Trilliums in haiku spirit). New Delhi: Imprint, 2007.

Songs Before Shrine. New Delhi: Authorspress, 2007.

This collection includes following four collections of poems earlier published:

——1. *Reflections & Wounds.* (poems) Hc. Vesta, 1978.

——2. *The Dove of Peace.* (poems) Pb., MAF Press, NY 1989, 1993.

——3. *Songs for Harmony.* (poems) Pb., Rose Shell Press, NJ, 1993.

——4.*Divergent Shades.* (poems) Xavier's College, India,1995.

——5. *The Flame.* Canada: Vesta Publications, 2008.

Fictional Works

Gill, Stephen. *Life's Vagaries* (short stories) . Vesta, 1974.

——*Why*. (a novel) Vesta, 1977.

——*The Loyalist City*. (a novel) Vesta, 1979.

——*Simon and the Snow King*. (children story, Illust.) Vesta, 1981.

——*Immigrant*. (a novel) Vesta, 1982.

——*The Blessings of a Bird*. (children story, illust) Vesta, 1983.

Critical Studies

Scientific Romances of H.G. Wells. Vesta, 1977.

Six Symbolist Plays of Yeats. Vesta, 1978.

Political Convictions of G.B. Shaw. Vesta, 1980.

Miscellaneous

The Discovery of Bangladesh. (history) Colin Venton, 1975.

Sketches of India (illust. essays about India). Vesta, 1988.

English Grammar for Beginners. Colin Venton, 1988.

Books in Urdu, Punjabi and Hindi

Aman Di Ghuggi. (Poems in Panjabi language) Publishers Cooperative, 1995.

Jazeera. (poems in Urdu) Vesta, 2005.

Jazeera .(poems in Hindi) Vesta, 2006.

Books Edited

Poets of the Capital. (Ottawa poets) Borealis Press, 1973.

Seaway Valley Poets . Vesta, 1975.

Green Snow: Anthology of Canadian Poets of Asian Origin. Vesta, 1976.

Tales from Canada for Children Everywhere. Vesta, 1979.

Anti-War Poems: Vol. 1. Vesta, 1984.

Anti-War Poems: Vol. 2nd . Vesta, 1986.

Vesta's Who's Who of North American Poets. Vesta, 1990.

Works in Translation

Zakhmi Perchawen (poems in Punjabi). Translator: Dr. Mohinder Kaur Gill. Hc., Suchinton Prakashan, New Delhi, India, 1980.

Reflexions Et Blessures (Poems in French). Trans. Roland Hamel, Vesta, 1979.

Awasi (Punjabi translation of his novel Immigrant). Translator: Balbir Momi. Pb., Pal Pocket Books, Amritsar, India, 1986.

Parwasi (translation of IMMIGRANT in Panjabi) Translators: Dr. N. Singh and S. Sarna. Pb., 1989. Vikendrit Group of Publications, Delhi, India.

Blessures (poems in French). Translator: Fr. Roland Hamel, Vesta, 1979.

Albums

Aman (Urdu / Hindi poems performed with music by a famous singer in a cassette). Released in 2003.

Aman Ki Rah (Urdu / Hindi poems performed with music by another famous signer from Pakistan). Released in 2005.

Selected Interviews of Dr. Stephen Gill (DVD album of about two hours). Released in 2005.

Website

http://www.stephengill.ca

Critical Material on Stephen Gill

Books on Stephen Gill

Glimpses (A Selection of published articles). Ed. Hamadan Derwesh, Canada: Vesta, 2005, revised in Fall 2008.

Hines, George. *Stephen Gill and His Works: An Evaluation.* New Delhi: Authors Press, 2007.

Discovering Stephen Gill: A Collection of Papers and Articles. (ed.) Dr. Nilanshu K. Agarwal . New Delhi: Authors press, 2008.

Arora, Sudhir K. *The Poetic Corpus of Stephen Gill: An Evaluation.* New Delhi: Sarup Book Publishers, 2009.

——*The Flame Unmasked: Stephen Gill's Epic Critically Examined.* (ed.) Bareilly, Prakash Book Depot, 2010.

Dominic, Savio G. *Trishanku Experiences in Stephen Gill's Immigrant* (forthcoming).

Research Papers, Book Reviews and Articles Published in Anthologies, Newspapers, Journals and Online Journals on Stephen Gill's Works

Agarwal, Alka. "Nature in Stephen Gill's *The Flame.*" *The Flame Unmasked: Stephen Gill's Epic Critically Examined* (ed.) Sudhir K. Arora. Bareilly: PBD, 2010: 154-164.

Agarwal, Nilanshu Kumar. "A Note on Stephen Gill's *The Flame*" http://www.stephengill.ca; Also in *Glimpses.* Vesta. 304-305.

——"A Critique of Stephen Gill's Literary Sensibility", *Discovering Stephen Gill: A Collection of Papers and Articles.* (ed.) Nilanshu Kumar Agarwal. New Delhi: Authorspress, 2008: 91-110.

——"Stephen Gill on His Writing and Diaspora: An Interview", *Discovering Stephen Gill: A Collection of Papers and Articles.* (ed.) Nilanshu Kumar Agarwal. New Delhi: Authorspress, 2008: 111-132.

Ahsan, Syed M. "Concept of Evil in Gill's Shrine", online *Pakistanchristianpost.com*; also *Glimpses*, Vesta, 2005:202-204.

Akhtar, Nilofar. "Stepher Gill's Immigrant: A Study in Diasporic Consciousness" *Discovering Stephen Gill: A Collection of Papers and Articles.* (ed.) Nilanshu Kumar Agarwal. New Delhi: Authorspress, 2008: 65-70.

Ansted University Educational Board. "Stephen Gill", online; *Cyber Literature* (India), vol. 9, June, 2002.

Arora, Sudhir K. "Indian Imagination in Stephen Gill's *The Flame*", *The Indian Journal of English Studies* vol. XLVI 2009 (ed.) The Association for English Studies of India. 219-228.

——"Stephen Gill's *The Flame*: Poetics of Peace", *Muse India.* www.museindia.com

——"Khalil Gibran and Stephen Gill: Prophets with Flames", *Bharat Times*. Montreal, April / May 2009: 16.

——"Tagore's Gitanjali and Stephen Gill's The Flame: A Comparative Study", *Bharat Times*. Montreal, June 2009: 16.

——"Stephen Gill's Muse: Humanitarian in Nature", *CanAsian Times*, Ottawa, July 4, 2009: 15.

——"Humanism in Stephen Gill's Poetry", *Literary Perspectives*. Vol. 4, NO. 2, July 2009: 78-84.

——"Stephen Gill's *The Flame* in the Light of the Theory of Rasa." *The Flame Unmasked: Stephen Gill's Epic Critically Examined* (ed.) Sudhir K. Arora. Bareilly: PBD, 2010: 25-41.

——"Prayers to the Flame: Stephen Gill and Niranjan Mohanty." *The Flame Unmasked: Stephen Gill's Epic Critically Examined* (ed.) Sudhir K. Arora. Bareilly: PBD, 2010: 102-114.

——"Stephen Gill's Craft in *The Flame*." *The Flame Unmasked: Stephen Gill's Epic Critically Examined* (ed.) Sudhir K. Arora. Bareilly: PBD, 2010: 195-212.

Balachandran, K. V. "Stephen Gill's *The Flame* at a Glance." *The Flame Unmasked: Stephen Gill's Epic Critically Examined* (ed.) Sudhir K. Arora. Bareilly: PBD, 2010: 140-144.

Bennett, Thea. "Yeats and Reincarnation", *Canadian India Times, The.* January 20, 1972.

Bhashyam. K. N. "All is not Rosy", *Hindu, The* (India), 15 May, 1979.

Boland, Viga. "Book of the Month", *Byword* (India), June, 1977.

——"Life's Vagaries and Wounds", *Medium* 11, vol. 2 #19, March 4, 1976.

——"Book of the Month (Green Snow)", *Byword* (India), July 1976.

——"Discovery", Canadian Authors and Bookman (Canada), Fall 1976.

Bratton, Daniel. "Introduction", *Discovering Stephen Gill: A Collection of Papers and Articles.* (ed.) Nilanshu Kumar Agarwal. New Delhi: Authorspress, 2008: vii.

Carter, Alixe, "Stephen Gill: writer, publisher but a doer first", *Ottawa Journal, The.* (daily, Canada), Saturday, October 29, 1977:26.

Chakravarthy, Tholana Ashok. "Stephen Gill: A Time-Tested Person With A Time-Trusted Vision", *Discovering Stephen Gill: A Collection of Papers and Articles.* (ed.) Nilanshu Kumar Agarwal. New Delhi: Authorspress, 2008: 157-158.

Chambial, D. C. "Songs for Harmony", *Poetcrit* (India), July 1999: 94.

——"Stephen Gill—Shrine", *Poetcrit* (India), January 2000:103-104.

Chauhan, G. S. "Who is Stephen Gill?" ed. Predesi Panjab; *Mashihi Sansar.* (March 15-31, 2003), *Daily Mehnat,* Jalandhar (Panjab), April 1, 2005; pakistanchristianpostonline. Feb. 28, 2003.

Choudhary, Arbind Kumar. "Stephen Gill in an interview with Dr. Arbind Kumar Choudhary, *Kohinoor* (India). No. 2, June 2008, vol. 4, pages 1-10.

Connell, Michelle D. "Gill's Shrine Implores To Think", *From Both Side of the Ocean* (USA). Sept.-October, 2000, no. 57

Darwesh, Hamadan. "A Study of Faiz Ahmed Faiz and Stephen Gill", *Glimpses*. Vesta, 2005: 238-247; *Jazeera* (Urdu collection of poems). Vesta 2004; several on line publications.

Dewar, Russ. "*Life's Vagaries*", from the introduction of *Life's Vagaries*. Vesta, 1974.

Dimitrov, Nikola. "Paradoxes in the Works of Stephen Gill", *Discovering Stephen Gill: A Collection of Papers and Articles*. (ed.) Nilanshu Kumar Agarwal. New Delhi: Authorspress, 2008: 71-76.

Dominic, K. V. "Stephen Gill's *The Flame*: An Epic on Anti-terrorism." *The Flame Unmasked: Stephen Gill's Epic Critically Examined* (ed.) Sudhir K. Arora. Bareilly: PBD, 2010: 115-128.

Drake, Bobbie. "Texas Poet Visits Dr. Gill", *India Globe, The* (USA), Dec. 1992.

——"Gill's The Flowers of Thirst", *India Globe, The* (USA), June 20, 1992.

Durrell, Robert. "Romances of H. G. Wells", *Temiskaming Speaker* (Canada). April 14, 1976.

——"Life's Vagaries", *Temiskaming Speaker* (Canada). May 12, 1976; Cornwall Weekly News, The, March 10, 1976, page 7.

——"Immigrant by Stephen Gill", *Nugget Book Reviews* (Canada). Feb. 16, 1979.

——"Why", *Nugget Focus* (Canada), January 13, 1978.

Dwivedi, A. N. "Fissures and Fractures": Identity Crisis in Gill's Poetry" *Discovering Stephen Gill: A Collection of Papers and Articles.* (ed.) Nilanshu Kumar Agarwal. New Delhi: Authorspress, 2008: 1-12.

Dwivedi, O. P. "Cross-cultural Conflicts in Stephen Gill's Immigrant" *Discovering Stephen Gill: A Collection of Papers and Articles.* (ed.) Nilanshu Kumar Agarwal. New Delhi: Authorspress, 2008: 77-82.

Educational Board of Ansted University. "Stephen Gill (Interview)," Online; *Cyber Literature* (India). vol. 9, June, 2002.

Elliot, Bianca. "Shrine", *Masihi Sansar* (Punjab, India). April 15, 2001, page 7; also *Kafla International* (Chandigarh, India). Sept.-Dec. 2001:25-26.

Fleischer, Denise. "Adds Another to Collection", *Gotta Write Network* (USA). Winter, 1991.

Fletcher, Peggy. "Alienation", *Canadian Author and Bookman.* vol. 51, no. 4, Summer 1976.

Gamble, Rick. "Literature Said Vital Force for World Peace", *Expositior, The* (daily, Canada). Sept. 8, 1976.

Gautam, G. L. "Triumph of the Flame: A Comparative Study of Shelley's *Triumph of life* and Stephen Gill's *The Flame.*" *The Flame Unmasked: Stephen Gill's Epic Critically Examined* (ed.) Sudhir K. Arora. Bareilly: PBD, 2010: 50-62.

Gill, K.S. "Poems of Social Consciousness", *South Asian Diary* (Canada). November 1, 2000.

Gill, Rashid. "Dr. Stephen Gill: A Born Poet of Peace" (Gill and Faiz comparison), ezine *pakistanchristianpost.com;* also *Glimpses.* Vesta, 2005.

Green, Mary. "Hard Work Pays Off", *Montreal Star, The* (Canada). Tuesday, Feb. 21, 1978.

Harper, A. W. J. "Struggle for Democracy", *London Free Press, The.* Saturday, June 18, 1977.

Heward, Burt. "Newcomer to Canada Shows How Publishing Can Survive", *Ottawa Citizen, The* (Canada). Tuesday, April 12, 1977.

Hitvada, The (India). "I'm Still Very Much an Indian", Tuesday, November 15, 1983.

Holt, Rochelle L. "A Call For Peace", *Pilot, The* (USA). January 20, 1992.

——"Anti-War Poems", *Small Press Review* (USA). August 1985.

Iverson, Ann. "Rainbow Strings: Hope in the Poetry of Dr. Stephen Gill", *Discovering Stephen Gill: A Collection of Papers and Articles.* (ed.) Nilanshu Kumar Agarwal. New Delhi: Authorspress, 2008: 139-140.

Journey. India (autobiographical), *Journal* (Canada). Dec. 25, 1998 and Jan. 1999

Keywan, Zonia. "Publisher Scorns Federal Handouts", *Gazette, The Daily* (Canada). Saturday, January 20, 1979.

Khatri, Chhote Lal. *Cyber Literature* (India). Dec. 1999:91-92.

——"Stephen Gill's *The Flame*: Symphony of Music, Imagery and Thought." *The Flame Unmasked: Stephen Gill's Epic Critically Examined* (ed.) Sudhir K. Arora. Bareilly: PBD, 2010: 91-101.

Koch, Terry. "Ideas Don't Report to Customs", *At Your Leisure* (USA). Sunday, April 9, 1978.

Kumar, Ashok and Roopali. "Stephen Gill's Life's Vagaries: A Critique" *Discovering Stephen Gill: A Collection of Papers and Articles.* (ed.) Nilanshu Kumar Agarwal. New Delhi: Authorspress, 2008: 49-52.

Kumar, Satish and Aunpam Bansal. 'The Flame of the *Bhagavadgita*: A Reading of Stephen Gill's *The Flame.*" *The Flame Unmasked: Stephen Gill's Epic Critically Examined* (ed.) Sudhir K. Arora. Bareilly: PBD, 2010: 129-139.

Lakhnavi, Prabhat Kumar Sarwar. "Peace in Sahir Ludhianvi and Stephen Gill", online: *Asian Tribune.* Blitz Internet Edition, and *pakistanchristianpost.*

Leitao, Lino. "Immigrant Novel: An Understanding of

Mankind", *Asian Tribune, The* (Canada). August 15, 1980, page 4.

——"The Concept of Harmony in the Ojibways of Canada and the Poetry of Stephen Gill", *Seva Bharati Journal of English Studies* (India). vol. 3, Feb. 2007:100-117. Also in *Pegasus* (India). Vol. VI, Jan-Dec., 2007: 40-56.

Linder, Norma West. "A Critical Study of H. G. Wells", *Link, The* (Canada). August 10, 1976.

——"Green Snow", *Samia Gazette* (Canada). August 11, 1976.

Locky, John Paul. "Stephen Gill: Poet and Protester for Peace", *Discovering Stephen Gill: A Collection of Papers and Articles.* (ed.) Nilanshu Kumar Agarwal. New Delhi: Authorspress, 2008: 141-143.

Long, Virginia Love. "Songs of Harmony", *Poetcrit* (India). 1997:61-63.

Lynch, Peggy Zuleika. "Fly on the Wall Interviews Presents Stephen Gill", *Poetry in The Arts Newsletter.* No. 23, January 2001; *Masihi Sansar* (India). January 31, 2001.

Manchanda, Madan. "Love is the Eternal Passion", *Pioneer, The* (India), Sunday, April 4, 1996.

Mahaheb International, The (Canada). "Stephen Gill's 1999 Literary Tour to India", April 1999: 28.

Marshall, Valerie (staff writer) "Writing time important for local writer-poet" *The Daily Standard-Freeholder* (Canada). Dec. 6. 1990.

Mishra, Arun Kumar. "Stephen Gill's *The Flame*: An Anatomy of Terrorism." *The Flame Unmasked: Stephen Gill's Epic Critically Examined* (ed.) Sudhir K. Arora. Bareilly: PBD, 2010: 165-177.

Mukhopadhyay, Aju. "Poet Stephen Gill: A Dreamer of Peace", *Discovering Stephen Gill: A Collection of Papers and Articles.* (ed.) Nilanshu Kumar Agarwal. New Delhi. Authorspress, 2008: 144-156.

pakistanchristianpost.com, "An Evening with Dr. Stephen Gill".

Parakot, Manjula. "Interesting Indians", *Canadian India Times* (Canada). Nov. 18, 1978.

Parameswari, D. "The Cultural Baggage: A Reading of Stephen Gill's *Immigrant*", online: *pakistanchristianpost.com; Glimpses.* Vesta, 2005.

Parameswari, D. "The Dialectics of Diasporic Experience: A Reading of Stephen Gill" *Discovering Stephen Gill: A Collection of Papers and Articles.* (ed.) Nilanshu Kumar Agarwal. New Delhi: Authorspress, 2008: 13-24.

Penny, Margaret. "Time is True Test for Writer's Ability", *Standard Freeholder,* The (daily Canada). October 19, 1975.

Philips, Bluebell S. "Gill Slide Stepped My Two-Step", *Asian Tribune* (Toronto, Canada).

——"Two Novels of Gill", *Asian Tribune, The* (Canada). October, 1979.

——"Wounds", Canadian India Times, The (Canada). September 19, 1974.

Preddie, Calvin. "Scholarly Work on Yeats", *Standard-Freeholder, The.* (daily, Canada), February 10, 1972.

Prime, Patricia. "*Shrine*: Poems of Social Concerns", *Mawaheb International* (Canada). June 2000: 4; *Canopy,* vol. xv 11 39 and 40, July 2000: 35-36.

Raja, P. "The Power of the Written Word: A Note on the Poetry of Stephen Gill", *Discovering Stephen Gill: A Collection of Papers and Articles.* (ed.) Nilanshu Kumar Agarwal. New Delhi: Authorspress, 2008: 133-138.

Raphael, Maryanne. "Gill's Poetry Enriches Life", *Bridge-in-Making* (India). Jan-Apr, 1998: 41-45.

Rasha, Miter. "A Multidimensional Person", *Perdesi Panjab* (Canada). Feb. 16, 1979 (originally appeared in Panjabi Language).

Ravichandran, T. "Green Dove in the Shrine: Ecoconcerns in Stephen Gill's Shrine", *Discovering Stephen Gill: A Collection of Papers and Articles.* (ed.) Nilanshu Kumar Agarwal. New Delhi: Authorspress, 2008: 25-34.

Reyes, Sophia. "A Hindu's Journey to Christian Faith", *Daily Standard Freeholder,* The (Canada). Sunday, July 23, 1994.

Robbins, John E. "Foreword" to Hines' *Stephen Gill and His Works.* New Delhi: Authorspress, 2008: v-vi.

Sahu, Antaryami. "Stephen Gill: A Poet of Peace and Harmony", online pakistanchristianpost.com, March 1, 2004; also *Bharat Times* (Canada). March 2004: 17.

Samal, S. "Eros in Gill's The Flowers of Thirst", *Writer's Lifeline* (Canada), 1992, No. 3.

——"Shrine", *Replica* (India), vol. 111, issue 1, January-March, 2000, pages 64-65.

——"Stephen Gill's Immaculate Articles", *Kafla International* (India). No. 20, Sept. - Dec. 1998: 39-47.

Sarangi, Jaydeep. "Interview with Stephen Gill", *Atlantic Literary Review, The* (India). July-Sept. and Oct.-Dec., 2004, vol. 5, no. 3-4, pages 164-183. Also published in *Inventing Ties and Bonds in English in Diasporic Literary Consciousness.* (ed.) Binod Mishra and P. J. Dhanasekaran. New Delhi: Authorspress 2008: 191-211.

——"Land and Identity in the Poetry of Stephen Gill and Jayanta Mahapatra", online pakistanchristianpost.com; also *Glimpses.* Vesta 2005. Also in *Inventing Ties and Bonds in English in Diasporic Literary Consciousness.* (ed.) Binod Mishra and P. J. Dhanasekaran. New Delhi: Authorspress 2008: 240-253.

Sass, Tish. "What Others Say", *Writer's Lifeline* (Canada). No. 5, 1986:28-30.

Saxena, Madhubala. "Human Beings minus Human Values: Maniac Messiahs in Stephen Gill's *The Flame.*" *The Flame Unmasked: Stephen Gill's Epic Critically Examined* (ed.) Sudhir K. Arora. Bareilly: PBD, 2010: 42-49.

Saxena, Sandhya. "Satan's Followers with Pandora's Box: A Comparative Study of *The Flame* and *Paradise Lost.*" *The Flame Unmasked: Stephen Gill's Epic Critically Examined* (ed.) Sudhir K. Arora. Bareilly: PBD, 2010: 12-24.

——"Multifarious Manifestations in Stephen Gill's*The Flame.*" *The Flame Unmasked: Stephen Gill's Epic Critically Examined* (ed.) Sudhir K. Arora. Bareilly: PBD, 2010: 63-75.

Saxena, Shweta. "Angst of Alienation in Stephen Gill's Poetry", *Discovering Stephen Gill: A Collection of Papers and Articles.* (ed.) Nilanshu Kumar Agarwal. New Delhi: Authorspress, 2008: 83-90.

——"Soication and Reghu in Gill's Immigrant: A Study" *Discovering Stephen Gill: A Collection of Papers and Articles.* (ed.) Nilanshu Kumar Agarwal. New Delhi: Authorspress, 2008: 35-48.

——"Battling Blazes in Stephen Gill's *The Flame.*" *The Flame Unmasked: Stephen Gill's Epic Critically Examined* (ed.) Sudhir K. Arora. Bareilly: PBD, 2010: 178-188.

Sharma, Anuradha. "Revamping Roles of Terrorism in *Ramcharitmanas* and *The Flame.*"

The Flame Unmasked: Stephen Gill's Epic Critically Examined (ed.) Sudhir K. Arora. Bareilly: PBD, 2010: 76-90.

Sharma, Brahama Dutt. "Stephen Gill As An Iconoclast" www.stephengill.ca; also in *Glimpses.* Vesta, 295-303.

Sharma. B. D. "Pacifism in Stephen Gill's Poetry" www.stephengill.ca

Sharma, Jagjit K. "New Books of Poems", *Star India* (Canada). May 14, 1993.

Shinghal, Ruchi. "Celebrating Peace: Stephen Gill's *The Flame.*" *The Flame Unmasked: Stephen Gill's Epic Critically Examined* (ed.) Sudhir K. Arora. Bareilly: PBD, 2010: 189-194.

Shukla, Rajesh. "Peace and Understanding", *Christian Monitor* (India). October 2, 1981.

Shukla, R. C. "The Speculative Solemnity in Stephen Gill's *The Flame." The Flame Unmasked: Stephen Gill's Epic Critically Examined* (ed.) Sudhir K. Arora. Bareilly: PBD, 2010: 1-11.

Singh, Kanwar Dinesh. "In the Fire of Self": A Critique of Stephen Gill's Shrine", *Discovering Stephen Gill: A Collection of Papers and Articles.* (ed.) Nilanshu Kumar Agarwal. New Delhi: Authorspress, 2008: 57-64.

Singh, Pritam. "Little Punjab in Canada", *Advance* (India). June 1990.

Singh, R. K. "Cross-cultural Communication", Language Forum (India), vol. xxxiv, no. 1-2, Jan-Dec. 1998; *Psychic Knot: Search for tolerance in Indian English Fiction.* Ed. R. K.Singh, Bahari Publications (India), 1998.

Singh, R. K. and Sarkar, Mitali De. "A Search for Elysium", *Mawaheb International, The* (Canada). June 1998.

Singh, S. "Sketches of India", *Writer's Lifeline* (Canada). July 1982.

Sinha, Bobbie. "Peace and Love", *Byword* (India). June-July, 1992.

Sinha, Ravi Nandan. From Introduction to Divergent Shades, 1995, *Writers' Forum.* Ranchi, India; also *Glimpses.* Canada: Vesta, 2005.

Skogsholm, Gunvor. "Fine Crafted Poetry", *Poetry Forum* (USA). January 1992.

Something about the Author. Something About the Author, vol. 63, pages 35-37, *Gale Research,* USA.

Srivastava K. K. "Firaq Gorakpuri and Stephen Gill as Poets" www.stephengill.ca; in *Contemporary Vibes.* July-Sep. 2008 and also in *Glimpses.* 306-313.

Suprovat Sarkar. "Poems by Stephen Gill", *Link, The* (Canada). Feb. 15 and March 1, 1975.

Tandon, N. K. "Discovery of Bangladesh", *Canadian India Times, The.* Dec. 11, 1975.

Tierney, Frank. "Reflection of an Indian Poet", *Canadian India Times, The* (Canada). Nov. 15, 1973.

Tripathy, Sailendra Narayan. "Seeking the Dove of Peace: The Poetry of Stephen Gill", *Discovering Stephen Gill: A Collection of Papers and Articles.* (ed.) Nilanshu Kumar Agarwal. New Delhi: Authorspress, 2008: 53-56.

Wadlow, Rene V. L. "Anti-War Poems", *Transnational Perspectives* (Switzerland). vol. 13, no. 3, 1987.

Wangu, J. L. "An Interview with a Canadian Author", *Indian Teacher, The* (India). Jan-Feb., 1979. vol. 1, No. 2.

Weerasinghe, Ashoka. "Foreword", *Discovering Stephen Gill: A Collection of Papers and Articles.* (ed.) Nilanshu Kumar Agarwal. New Delhi: Authorspress, 2008: v

Westcott, W. F. "Immigrant", *Christian Monitor* (India). November 2, 1980.

Wiles, Clifton A. "The Flowers of Thirst", *al-mohajer* (Canada). No. 4, April, 1994.

Wouk, Judith. "Children's Stories: A Companion", *Writer's Lifeline* (Canada). 1986, number 3.

Index